STRATEGY FORMULATION
Power and Politics
Second Edition

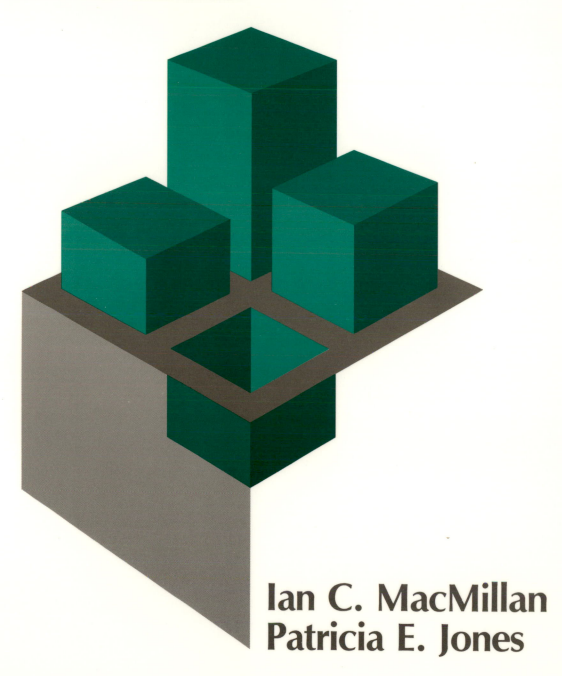

Ian C. MacMillan
Patricia E. Jones

STRATEGY FORMULATION

THE WEST SERIES IN STRATEGIC MANAGEMENT

Consulting Editor
Charles W. Hofer

Setting Startegic Goals and Objectives, 2d ed.
Max D. Richards

Strategy Formulation: Issues and Concepts
Charles W. Hofer

Strategy Formulation: Power and Politics, 2d ed.
Ian C. MacMillan and Patricia E. Jones

Strategy Implementation: Structure, Systems, and Process, 2d ed.
Jay R. Galbraith and Robert K. Kazanjian

Strategic Control
Peter Lorange, Michael F. Scott Morton, and Sumantra Ghoshal

Macroenvironmental Analysis for Strategic Management
Liam Fahey and V. K. Narayanan

Second Edition

STRATEGY FORMULATION
POWER AND POLITICS

Ian C. MacMillan
NEW YORK UNIVERSITY

Patricia E. Jones
MANAGEMENT CONSULTANT

WEST PUBLISHING COMPANY

St. Paul   New York   Los Angeles   San Francisco

Copyediting by Joan Torkildson

Interior art by Alice B. Thiede, Carto-Graphics

Cover design by Peter Thiel, Kim Rafferty

Typesetting by Huron Valley Graphics, Inc. Typefaces are Aster and Optima.

Index prepared by Lois Oster

Library of Congress Cataloging-in-Publication Data

MacMillan, Ian C. 1940–

Strategy formulation.

(The West series in strategic management)
Bibliography:
Includes index.
1. Strategic planning. 2. Organizational behavior.
3. Interorganizational relations I. Jones,
Patricia E. II. Title.
HD30.28.M283 1986   658.4'012   85–20389
ISBN 0–314–85260–3

CONTENTS

8

Illustrative Case Study:
Alpha Oil Mills   *111*

9

Illustrative Case Study:
A. Bailey (Pty), Ltd.   *121*

10

Illustrative Case Study:
Apollo Wholesalers   *136*

11

Illustrative Case Study:
Herbicide Division of
Mid-West Chemical Company   *148*

References   *153*

Index   *157*

FOREWORD

This series is a response to the rapid and significant changes that have occurred in the strategic management/business policy area over the past twenty-five years. Although strategic management/ business policy is a subject of long standing in management schools, it was traditionally viewed as a capstone course whose primary purpose was to *integrate* the knowledge and skills students had gained in the functional diciplines. During the past fifteen years, however, strategic management/business policy has developed a substantive content of its own. Originally, this content focused on the concepts of corporate and business strategies and on the processes by which such strategies were formulated and implemented within organizations. More recently, as Figure 1 and Table 1 illustrate, the scope of the field has broadened to include the study of both the functions and responsibilities of top management and the organizational systems and processes used to establish overall organizational goals and objectives and to formulate, implement, and control the strategies and policies necessary to achieve these goals and objectives.

When the *West Series in Business Policy and Planning* was originally published, most of the texts in the field did not yet reflect this extension in scope. The principal purpose of the original series was, therefore, to fill this void by incorporating the latest research findings and conceptual thought in the field into each of the texts in the series. In the intervening seven years, the series has succeeded to a far greater degree than we could have ever hoped.

However, the pace of research in strategic management/business policy has, if anything, increased since the publication of the original series. Some changes are, thus, clearly in order. It is the purpose of the *West Series in Strategic Management* to continue the tradition

**Figure 1   The Evolution of
Business Policy/Strategic Management as a Field of Study**

The Traditional Boundary of Business Policy

The
Functions and
Responsibilities
of General
Management

The
Strategic
Processes
of the
Organization

The Current Boundaries of Strategic Management

Some Major Contributors to the Redefinition of the Field

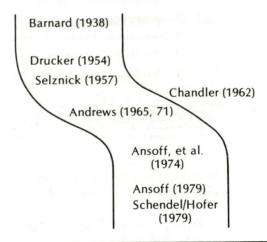

Barnard (1938)

Drucker (1954)

Selznick (1957)

Chandler (1962)

Andrews (1965, 71)

Ansoff, et al.
(1974)

Ansoff (1979)
Schendel/Hofer
(1979)

of innovative, state-of-the-art coverage of the field of strategic management started by the *West Series in Business Policy and Planning* both through revisions to all the books in the original series, and through the addition of two new titles. In making such revisions, care has been taken to ensure not only that the various texts fit together as a series, but also that each is self-contained and addresses a major topic in the field. In addition, the series has been designed so that it covers almost all the major topics that form the

Table 1   The Major Subfields of Business Policy/Strategic Management

    1. Boards of Directors

    2. The Nature of General Management Work

    3. Middle-Level General Management

*   4. Stakeholder Analysis

    5. Organizational Goal Formulation

    6. Corporate Social Policy and Management Ethics

*   7. Macroenvironmental Analysis

✔   8. Strategy Formulation and Strategic Decision Making

    9. Corporate-Level Strategy (including Mergers, Acquisitions, and Divestitures)

  10. Business-Level Strategy

  11. Strategic Planning and Information Systems

  12. The Strategy-Structure-Performance Linkage

  13. The Design of Macroorganizational Structure and Systems

  14. Strategic Control Systems

* 15. Organizational Culture

  16. Leadership Style for General Managers

  17. The Strategic Management of Small Businesses and New Ventures

  18. The Strategic Management of High Tech Organizations

  19. The Strategic Management of Not-for-Profit Organizations

✔ Indicates subfields that are covered extensively by this text

* Indicates other subfields that are discussed in this text

heartland of strategic management, as Figure 2 illustrates. The individual texts in the series are

Setting Strategic Goals and Objectives, 2d ed.
Max D. Richards

Strategy Formulation: Issues and Concepts
Charles W. Hofer

Strategy Formulation: Power and Politics, 2d ed.
Ian C. MacMillan and Patricia E. Jones

Strategy Implementation: Structure, Systems, and Process, 2d ed.
Jay R. Galbraith and Robert K. Kazanjian

Strategic Control
Peter Lorange, Michael F. Scott Morton, and Sumantra Ghoshal

Macroenvironmental Analysis for Strategic Management
Liam Fahey and V. K. Narayanan

Figure 2   The Strategic Management Process

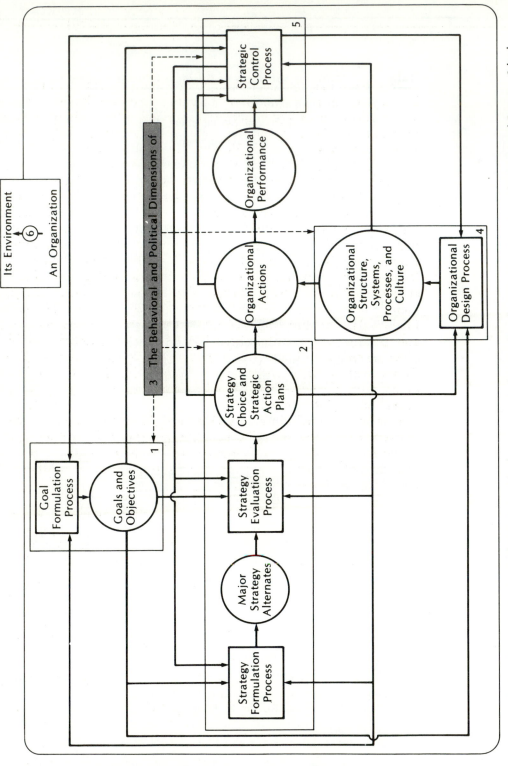

1. Setting Strategic Goals and Objectives, 2d ed.

2. Strategy Formulation: Issues and Concepts

3. Strategy Formulation: Power and Politics, 2d ed.

4. Strategy Implementation: Structure, Systems, and Process, 2d ed.

5. Strategic Control

6. Macroenvironmental Analysis for Strategic Management

The series has also been designed so that the texts within it can be used in several ways. First, the entire series can be used as a set to provide an advanced conceptual overview of the field of strategic management. Second, selected texts in the series can be combined with cases drawn from the Harvard Case Services, the Case Teaching Association, and/or the Case Research Association to create a course customized to particular instructor needs. Third, individual texts in the series can be used to supplement the conceptual materials contained in the existing text and casebooks in the field. The series thus offers the individual instructor great flexibility in designing the required business policy/strategic management course. Fourth, because of their self-contained nature, each of the texts can be used either individually or in combination with other materials as the basis for an advanced specialized course in strategic management. For instance, the text on the "Strategic Control Systems." Likewise, the *Macroenvironmental Analysis for Strategic Management* and *Strategy Formulation: Power and Politics* texts could be combined to create an innovative course on "Stakeholder Management." Or the text on *Setting Strategic Goals and Objectives* could be combined with a text on boards of directors to create an advanced course on the latter topic.

Finally, in concluding this Common Foreword I would like to thank my co-editor on the original series, Dan Schendel of Purdue University, for his efforts on that series. They were both substantial and valuable. Indeed, the series could not have been established as effectively as it was without him.

Charles W. Hofer
Editor
October 1985

PREFACE

This textbook is intended for both practicing managers and business management students. It provides a framework for thinking about strategy with a political perspective. The thrust of the argument is that managers, as strategists, must take into account the behavioral and political components of internal and external stakeholders when they formulate strategies in order to ensure the success of the organizations they manage.

The text is structured in such a way that the initial chapters are rich in concept. This conceptual material is systematically developed into a practical framework for political strategy formulation, so that, by the end of the book, the whole focus is on practical application. In the last part of the text, four case studies are analyzed thoroughly to show the applicability of the theory.

To avoid cumbersome references within the text, the source material on which the reasoning was based is listed in a bibliography at the end of the text. Those interested in pursuing specific topics in more depth should refer to the works listed. These works have been held to a minimum.

The intent of the textbook is to provide a broad delineation of the field of political strategy. The reader should emerge in the end with some systematic concepts about formulating political strategy. These should complement the approaches to economic strategy formulation that have been discussed in the other books in the *West Series in Strategic Management*.

We wish to express our gratitude to the following people: Henry Lowenstein, University of Illinois-Chicago, Marilyn L. Taylor, University of Kansas, William H. Newman, Columbia University

1

Introduction

THE PURPOSE OF THIS TEXT

Let us broadly define political behavior as that part of human behavior which seeks to get others to do what we want, when they might not elect to do so. In the context of this definition, this book is designed to help students and practitioners of business policy develop an understanding of the political components of business behavior and organizational strategy. However, it is also possible to apply the concepts in the text to contexts outside of business. The principles that will be discussed here have been applied to hospitals, church groups, and many nonprofit organizations, as well as to other groups.

The book is intended to complement the writings of the other authors in the West Series in Strategic Management. Due to the nature of the topics, there is some overlap; however, this book assiduously tries to avoid repetition of the work on business strategies by Hofer and Schendel, on organizational goals by Richards, on strategy implementation by Galbraith and Kazanjian, and on environmental analysis by Fahey and Narayanan.

The focus of this text is on politics, intraorganizational and interorganizational. The models are intended to be pragmatic and useful for general managers in their efforts to balance the demands being pressed on them by disparate, and perhaps powerful, interest groups inside and outside the organization. Without denying the importance of the individual's personal values, the text leaves such discussion to the well-researched literature in the behavioral sciences. Use of the concepts in this book will increase the chances of successful strategy implementation by explicitly addressing the *politics* of implementation during the formulation process itself.

1

THE POLITICAL PERSPECTIVE

Why Political Strategy?

With the increased emphasis in the last two decades on strategic planning, most managers are capable of formulating strategies that are, as much as any forecast can be, *technically* correct. Why then has implementation been such a problem?

The answer to this question is a simple one: Too often the strategist has failed to anticipate organizational politics and build it into the formulation process. All organizations are political systems, made up of politically active individuals. To accomplish individual strategy, one is often *compelled* to have people act in ways they otherwise might not, particularly those key stakeholders on whom one's strategy depends. Failure to identify who these key stakeholders are and to anticipate and manage their behavior can drastically slow down strategy execution if not render it impossible. Strategy formulation *must* include the *political plan:* how one intends to manage the key stakeholders.

This book is concerned with how these stakeholders behave and how such behavior can be predicted. It looks at strategic decision-making as a complex behavioral process in which the decisions of the strategist are interrelated with the decisions and motivation of the other key players inside or outside the organization.

Three Behavioral Models

Our book draws heavily on the perspectives of Allison (1971). He discusses the ways in which complex strategic decisions are made from the perspective of three distinct, but not mutually exclusive models: the rational actor model, the organizational process model, and the bureaucratic politics model. While Allison's focus was on decision-making, the models offer behavioral insights that are helpful for the analysis and subsequent management of key stakeholders.

With the *rational actor* model, conceive of the stakeholders as a rational, unitary decision maker with a clear set of goals, who perceives options clearly, generates a clear sense of alternative actions, and selects the alternative on a rational basis.

With the *organizational process* model, consider the stakeholder as comprising a group of departments held together in the organization and coordinated by a series of rules, procedures, policies, and programs. The decisions that the organization makes will be determined by the particular perspectives of the different departments, each with their own narrow perspective on the problem, their own set of goals, and their own desired choices. It may not be possible for the organization to perceive the whole problem but only parts of it, depending on the perceptions of the various departments. For instance, a strategic move that we make to secure control of a specific segment in the market, such as the "youth market," may influence sales of the product marginally over many geographic areas. If the competitors monitor sales by geographic region only, each geographic division tracking its sales over time, then the overall impact on their total sales may be small enough to be dismissed as a temporary aberration in sales. Further, if these figures are collated only by quarter, it may take several months before they are even aware of our inroads. In the meantime, we may have had the opportunity to consolidate our position.

The *bureaucratic politics* model views the stakeholder as a series of coalitions in the organization, each with a leader who has to represent the interests of the coalition. Decision-making is thus characterized by political perspectives as each coalition leader views the possible alternative action in terms of how it will affect the power and influence structure of the organization and the impact on the leader as a member of the coalition, as a member of the organization, and as a person.

All the previous perspectives are useful when attempting to anticipate stakeholder reactions to strategic moves and, consequently, formulate strategies for managing their behavior. The remainder of this book deals with specific areas for analysis and resultant implications for action—in other words, getting key actors inside and outside the firm to do what they otherwise might not do.

AN OUTLINE OF THIS TEXT

The directions of the argument in this text can be followed by referring to Figure 1.1, which is a much-simplified outline of the material to be discussed in this textbook. As a result of the environmental analysis (discussed by Hofer and Schendel 1978), the organization perceives certain *threats and opportunities*. As we have said, the first step in the political approach is to carry out a systems analysis to determine who the *key stakeholders* are who influence these threats and opportunities. Organizations that pose threats are potential targets of the organization. Organizations that will benefit from opportunities become potential allies of the organization.

The political strategy formulation approach recognizes that

Figure 1.1   Schematic Outline of Political Strategy Formulation

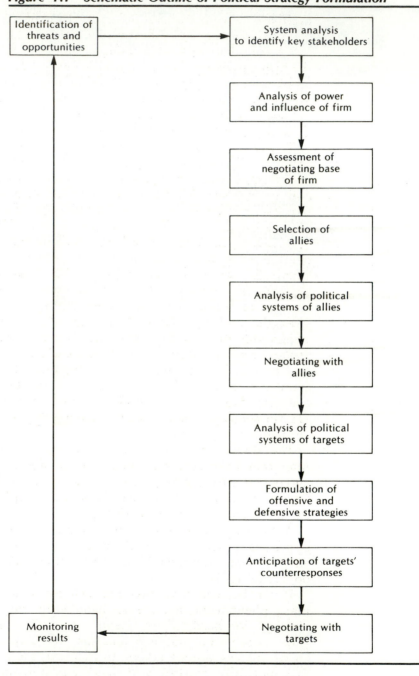

where it is legal, the firm will seek out these allies to help achieve its goals. At the beginning of this political strategy approach, determining the relative *power and influence* of the firm is necessary. On the basis of its power and influence, the firm can find a sense of what it can accomplish without forming an alliance. With this knowledge, the firm can determine its *negotiating base* —the minimum it will be prepared to accept when it forges a negotiated alliance with its allies. The negotiating base provides the foundation for a negotiating strategy by which the firm can go out and form an alliance with those organizations that can assist it in achieving its goals.

The firm therefore *selects potential allies* and then carries out a detailed internal and external *political systems analysis* of its allies to determine what *their* power and influence are and what strengths and weaknesses *they* have. The firm then carries out *negotiations* that result in the formulation of an alliance. If this is successful, the alliance can turn its attention to potential targets.

As before, the internal and external stakeholders are analyzed to develop an idea of what the *targets'* power and influence are and where *their* strengths and weaknesses lie. This analysis provides the basis for the formulation of *offensive strategies*, aimed at taking advantage of those opportunities in which the alliance can use its strengths, and *defensive strategies*, aimed at avoiding or countering weaknesses that reinforce the threats facing the alliance. As these strategies are identified, the alliance can anticipate what *counterresponses* can be expected from the targets. Some strategies can be countered easily; others can be more difficult for the targets to counter. Thus, a best set of offensive and defensive strategies can be determined, and the strategic counterresponses of targets to these strategies determined.

The alliance then launches its offensive and defensive strategies. After they have been launched, it is often necessary to come to an agreement with the targets to avoid mutually destructive conflict. Hence, a negotiating strategy must be formulated to prepare for these critical *negotiations with targets*.

After the strategies have been launched, the progress of these strategies is monitored and the results are then used to reinitiate the environmental analysis. Thus, the identification of new threats and opportunities is achieved.

It can be seen that this approach requires the investigation of many phenomena that are not handled in traditional textbooks on strategy. We need to pay attention to such topics as power, influence, negotiation, political analysis, and anticipation of strategic countermoves, among others. In this text, these topics are explored systematically, starting with basic and fundamental concepts and developing into fairly elaborate models with a deliberately political perspective.

In Chapter 2, the concept of manipulation is explained. We try to unfold what such phenomena as power, influence, and authority really mean. Given these insights, we try to explain what the bases of power and influence are. How does one become influential? What contributes to power? With the answers to these questions, it is possible to formulate guidelines for developing power and influence that can be used to structure the behavior of targets so that the organization can achieve its ends.

In Chapter 3, the discussion focuses upon negotiation. In particular, we look at win-win negotiating. Tactics for handling such situations are developed, and the tactics of bluffing, threatening, and promising are analyzed in detail. Then, attention is given to the development of a negotiating strategy, which focuses on the entire negotiation process and integrates the various bluffs, threats, and promises that are required to handle each issue that arises in a complex negotiation.

Chapter 4 examines the behavior of an individual within a complex organization. From this political model of individual behavior is traced the formation of coalitions and interest groups in organizations.

Chapter 5 highlights external stakeholder relations. The various political moves that an organization can take under different environmental structures are identified. At the end of the section, guidelines for developing a political thrust in different environments are suggested. Then, attention is given to the problem of strategic anticipation: What responses can targets make to an organization's strategies, and which responses are they likely to make? Several guidelines for strategic anticipation are provided.

In Chapter 6, the whole process of policy formulation and execution in a political structure within the organization is developed. The importance of this model for political strategy—in the process of manipulating or accommodating the environment (or both) to achieve corporate goals—is discussed.

Chapter 7 turns to the concept of political strategy formulation—the formulation of a manipulative or accommodative strategy (or both) that will so structure conditions in the organization's environment that the corporate strategy is achieved. A broad set of guidelines is developed that elaborates upon the outline given in Figure 1.1.

In Chapters 8, 9, 10, and 11, four cases are discussed. Specific facets of the political strategy formulation process are highlighted in the analysis of these cases, which are used to illustrate the application of many of the principles explained in this text.

A NOTE ON ETHICS

It should be noted that there is a danger that these concepts can be used unethically. While we are concerned with bad ethics, we can prescribe no specific ethical stance. It is not for us to dictate ethics to readers. Our purpose is to explore phenomena that have been observed in practice but have been underemphasized in theory until now. We draw many disguised examples from practice to illustrate the concepts. These examples are neither condoned nor condemned; they are all real-life examples observed in practice and reported as such. Readers have their own set of ethics, but in reading this book, they should recognize that the concepts discussed in this text can be used *without overstepping any personal ethical limits.*

2

Power and Influence

In this chapter, we investigate manipulation (in its positive connotation) and the two routes available to the manipulator: power and influence. With regard to power and influence, the major emphasis here is on the sources available to the formulator of strategy for operational use, not on the origins and use of *personal* power. Personal power, while an important concept, is discussed in depth in other works (see French and Raven 1968) and is not duplicated here. The discussion of individual political behavior presented in Chapter 4 is sufficient for the focus of the book. The reasoning in the following sections comes mainly from the work of Chamberlain (1955), Rappaport (1960), Thompson (1967), Blau (1969), Parsons (1969), Pettigrew (1973), Tushman (1977), Pfeffer (1981), and Tichy (1983).

MANIPULATION

It is not without trepidation that we use the term *manipulation*, due to its generally negative connotation. However, it is also a reality that cannot be denied or ignored. Whether one calls it manipulation, behavior shaping, or positioning, the concept is the same; that is, getting other individuals, departments, or organizations to do something they might otherwise not do. In its positive sense, manipulation was practiced by Moses, Christ, Mohammed, Buddha, and Confucius, as well as by many other respected world leaders. Specifically, manipulation is the unilateral activity undertaken by a political player to get a target to behave as the player wishes. (This is in contrast to accommodative action, in which the player takes action with the intent of coming to *joint agreement* with the target as to how the player and the target will behave.) Note that we use the noun *target* rather than *opponent*. From the discussion and examples that follow, you will see that manipulation does not necessarily imply a winner and a loser (or victim!). Chapter 3 suggests methods of manipulation to ensure a win-win negotiating strategy in which the underlying purpose of the action is to achieve agreements that benefit *all* parties.

Manipulation is accomplished by the player restructuring the environment in such a way that the target *decides* on a course of action desirable to the player. The key to manipulation lies in intervening in the target's decision-making process.

In deciding on a course of action, people assess the effects of alternate courses of action on their aspirations. Everyone has some structure of aspirations against which they compare the alternatives. Targets will judge the positive and negative connotations of each of the alternatives being considered and, on their specific personal basis, develop some sense of personal satisfaction with the outcomes of the alternatives. The alternative with the highest level of satisfaction will then be selected.

A simple two-alternative situation is illustrated in Figure 2.1: A child must choose between doing homework and going to the movies. Both alternatives have both positive and negative connotations for him. Doing homework means that he gets approval from parents and teachers and increases his chances of getting a high grade. However, he may find homework boring and tiresome. Going to the movies promises to be enjoyable and exciting, but it costs part of his allowance and leaves him with feelings of guilt afterward. In the absence of intervention by a manipulative player, he will weigh the alternatives in terms of *his own* assessment of the positive and negative connotations of each alternative. Let us suppose that the balance of these results in measures of satisfaction that lie at A and B on his scale of increasing satisfaction in Figure 2.1.

Figure 2.1   Simple Two-Alternative Example

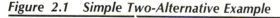

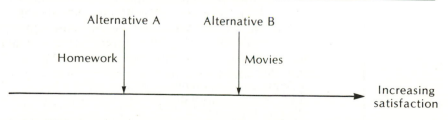

B clearly lies at a higher level of satisfaction than A, so he will elect to go to the movies. If his parents decide to manipulate this situation, they must intervene in the process and cause him to select the alternative that best suits them. There are four ways of doing this, which are explored next.

Channels of Manipulation

The target makes decisions on the basis of his perception of the environment surrounding him. We can conceive of two possible channels[1] for getting him to rerank the alternatives and select the alternative we desire.

Situation Channel.   First, we can change the structure of the situation in which he is placed. In the light of this changed situation, he may decide on a course of action that he would otherwise not have chosen. In other words, by rearrangement of the things or people in the situation itself, the structure of the situation is changed, and this restructuring results in manipulated action.

Intentional Channel.   Alternatively, we can attempt to change the target's intentions, not by restructuring the situation but by communicating with him in such a way that his perceptions of the situation change. In the light of his changed perception, he may change his intentions and decide on a new course of action that he would otherwise not have chosen (see Figure 2.2).

Modes of Manipulation

We have another dimension by which to structure these decision alternatives, namely, the use of positive and negative modes of action.

If we use the positive mode, then the target feels better off as a result of the manipulation. If we use a negative mode, then he feels worse off. These situations are illustrated in Figures 2.2 and 2.3. In

---

1. While the two channels identified here are the same at the psychological level, this method of differentiating between types of action proves useful at the political level.

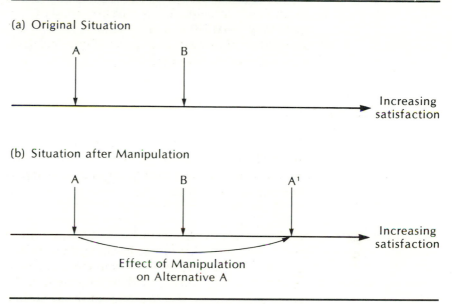

Figure 2.2   Positive Mode of Manipulation

(a) Original Situation

A   B

Increasing
satisfaction

(b) Situation after Manipulation

A   B   A¹

Increasing
satisfaction

Effect of Manipulation
on Alternative A

Figure 2.2, the positive mode is illustrated. In the first part of the figure, the original situation is depicted. Clearly, the target would choose alternative action B over action A. However, the manipulator would prefer that action A be selected. In the second part of Figure 2.2, the situation after the manipulator has intervened by using the positive mode is shown. In some way or another, alternative A has been moved to A^1. And the target will select A^1 and at the same time feel better off, because the level of satisfaction of choosing the desired action A^1 is higher than the original level of satisfaction of the original best alternative B.

The negative mode of manipulation is shown in Figure 2.3. In the first part, the target would choose action B rather than action A. However, the manipulator would prefer him to choose action A. In the second part of the figure, the position after the manipulator has acted in a negative mode is depicted.

The manipulator has caused the satisfaction associated with action B to move down to B^1, and the target will select action A but will feel worse off, since the outcome is less satisfactory to him than before the manipulative action.

Having identified two channels and two modes of manipulative action, we can now combine these dimensions and identify and label four major means of manipulation.

Figure 2.3   Negative Mode of Manipulation

(a) Original Situation

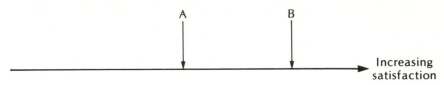

(b) Situation after Manipulation

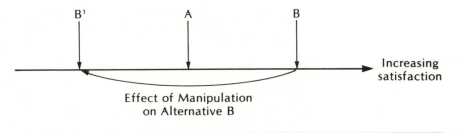

Four Means of Manipulation

The two dimensions combined produce four general ways of manipulating a target (See Table 2.1).

Inducement.   The manipulator attempts to change the structure of the situation, so that the target's circumstances are improved by the selection of the alternative desired.

■ For instance, suppose a manager wanted to quit her job to join another organization. The boss could offer her a large salary increase to make her stay. If the manager decides to stay, she has been induced by the offer of extra salary and will feel better off as a result of doing so. Her feelings toward the manipulation will be positive.

Coercion.   The manipulator atttempts to change the situation's structure, so that the target's circumstances are aggravated by not selecting the alternative desired.

■ For instance, suppose the manager wanted to quit, and the boss threatened to get court injunctions preventing her from leaving because of an employment contract she signed, or suppose the boss threatened to

Table 2.1   Four Means of Manipulation

Mode	Channel	
	Situational	*Intentional*
Positive	Inducement	Persuasion
Negative	Coercion	Obligation

blacklist her from the industry. The manager might decide to stay but would feel worse off as a result. Her feelings toward the manipulation would be negative.

Persuasion.   The manipulator does not attempt to change the situation but presents arguments and logic to the target, showing that acting as the manipulator desires corresponds better with the target's achievement of satisfaction than the target originally perceived. If the manipulator is successful, the target will commit herself to the desired alternative and feel that she has gained by doing so.

■ For instance, if the manager in the previous example announced her intention to quit, and the boss started to argue that the real challenge for managers lies in the present organization and that anyone staying with the organization would virtually be guaranteed a successful future, and so on, he might be able to persuade the manager that it is better to stay with the present organization. If this persuasive argument were successful, the manager would feel that she has benefited by the decision to stay and would feel positive about the manipulation.

Obligation.   The manipulator directs to the target logic or argument that shows that the target's original perception of the alternatives was not correct and that the alternative that she was considering selecting was not in keeping with the values she holds. If the attempt is successful, the target selects the alternative the manipulator desires, but feels worse off as a result. As much as she might wish to select the original alternative, she now feels obligated to select the alternative the manipulator desires.

■ For instance, the manager's boss might make the manager feel obligated to stay with the present organization because her present employers have invested a great deal of money and effort in training her in the skills for which she has been offered the new job. Though she might feel obligated to stay, she would be somewhat unhappy about doing so.

These four means of manipulation are presented in abstract, pure form for discussion purposes only. In practice, a manipulator might try combinations of these means to effect the desired responses on the part of the target. Note that where there is an option, changed perceptions are usually more difficult to erode by counterattack and are therefore more desirable than changing the situation. Using the positive mode results in fewer negative aftereffects (e.g., resentment, sabotage) and is therefore more desirable than the negative mode. However, these four means of manipulation do help clarify what is being attempted in a manipulation and, in particular, allow for more precise definitions of power and influence than are obtained in everyday language.

The degree of manipulative success enjoyed by an actor depends on the degree to which he is able to either restructure situations or restructure perceptions. In the following sections we use these concepts to define power and influence and discuss strategies for building bases of each.

POWER

Power is regarded as the capacity of an actor (person, group, organization, nation) in a particular situation to manipulate via the structural channel. That is, power is the manipulator's ability to *restructure the situation* in such a way as to get others to act as he desires.

Two things are worth noting about this definition. First, power is situationally determined. That is, one's power is a function of the *situation:* Power in one situation (at work) does not necessarily mean power in another situation (at home). Second, power is a capacity: One does not have to use power to have it. The mere recognition of the power of an actor by his targets affects the moves that they consider, so the actor need not necessarily exercise that capacity to have an effect on their actions.

INFLUENCE

Influence is, in contrast, defined as the ability of a manipulator to *restructure perceptions* of targets in a situation, to get them to act as desired. Like power, influence is situationally determined. Like power, too, influence can be a capacity. The recognition of influence capacity of an actor by his targets will affect the moves that they consider without the actor having to actually exercise that influence. Banks for example, are inclined to consider the views of the president's economic adviser (who has influence, not power) before changing rates or policies.

SOURCES OF POWER

The basis of power rests in the ability to restructure situations. The work of writers such as Emerson (1962), Thompson (1967), Blau (1969), and Crozier (1971) suggests that there are four strategies for gaining power: possession of strategic resources, control of alternatives, leveraging existing influence, and the use of authority. We will discuss each in turn.

Possession of Strategic Resources

If one is to restructure a situation, one needs the resources to do so, and since power is situation specific, the resources required are situation specific. Therefore, it is pointless to try to list all the possible resources that could be important sources of power. Almost any resource could, in specific circumstances, be an important power resource.

Instead, it is useful to unfold the *characteristics* of the resource that makes it a power resource in a specific situation. Then, by analysis of a situation, one can determine which resources are or will be important determiners of the power base.

Five characteristics are useful in the identification of power resources:

1. need
2. scarcity
3. deployability
4. convertibility
5. timing

In other words, the resource not only must be one that is *needed* by the target of the power play but also must be a *scarce* resource (we all need air, but seldom is it scarce). If all players have ready access to it, its possibilities as a power resource are nil.

It is also important to realize that a power resource must be *deployable* to the situation. Resources are deployed to induce or to coerce. If the resource cannot be used either to induce or coerce or to resist inducement or coercion from the target, then it is not valuable as a power base.

■ For instance, all the sophisticated, modern military equipment (such as supersonic fighters) of advanced nations is not appropriate to guerrilla warfare in dense jungles. In such a situation, a small group of dedicated fighters who are prepared to live under the most debilitating conditions could be a more important resource.

■ Similarly, resources such as production capacity and stockpiles of raw materials are not useful to a firm that is in the throes of an industry recession, but are useful in the middle of an industry boom.

The last example allows us to introduce two other concepts that are important in assessing the value of resources as a power base: *convertibility* and *timing*.

Production capacity is often far more difficult to convert into other resources (such as cash) than, say, raw material stockpiles. Thus, it is convertibility, coupled with timing, that determines the strategic nature of power resources.

■ For instance, in many smaller economies, the building industry suffers chronic shortages. The companies that are able to convert their resources in time to meet these shortages tend to prosper, and those that cannot tend to founder. A typical pattern might be as follows. There is an under-supply of cement during a boom. Companies scramble to secure cement, only to find that supply sources are committed to the more aggressive and far-thinking competitors. After losing a great deal of business and incurring heavy expenses securing cement supplies, the companies find that there is now adequate cement but a shortage of skilled labor—they have the material but not the labor. Having gotten the labor, there is a shortage of funds to support working capital. In each case, it takes a great deal of effort to obtain the strategic resources required at the time. It must be done by converting existing resources, that are not strategically valuable, to resources that are.

Generally, a resource is strategic in a power context when there is an undersupply (or close to it) and when it is difficult or costly for various competitors to convert existing resources into the strategic resource.

■ Thus, crude oil became a strategic resource only after the OPEC producers deliberately withheld supplies and when the industrial nations were in the middle of an arduous winter. There was no way they could convert to other sources of energy. If alternative energy sources are ever developed, oil will no longer be a strategic resource in international economies. As less energy is consumed, oil becomes less scarce and so loses its strategic value as a power resource. Until alternatives are *freely* available, however, it is going to remain a significant strategic resource.

To summarize, the key concept to bear in mind concerning possession of resources as a power base is that such resources must be needed, scarce, deployable to the situation, and difficult to obtain by conversion of other resources without delay or great costs. It is important to note that the power resource need not be materials. Such things as a pool of high-quality management talent or R&D skills could be important power resources.

Control of Alternatives

A second facet to the structure of strategic resources is in the structure of available alternatives. Suppose there is one person in the entire country who is qualified to carry out a certain job. Suppose also that there is only one organization that needs the qualifications of this person but that they need her in order to operate.

The question is, Who has the power in this situation? The answer is that the person and the organization both have power over one another. The person can do a great deal of harm to the organization by not cooperating, so she has some basis for coercion by the fact that she possesses unique skills that are desired by the organization. At the same time, the organization has a basis of coercion in that it is uniquely needed as a place of employment for the skilled person. They both have power, but it tends to be balanced.

What happens when there are two people with these skills and only one organization? We sense immediately that the organization has more power than either of the individuals, because it has more alternatives than they do. Unless the individuals can get together and form a coalition (which is discussed in Chapter 4), thus reducing the alternatives available to the organization, the organization can induce or coerce one or both of the individuals to do its bidding far more easily than in the case of the one-to-one relationship.

The structure of alternatives available to an organization and its targets is an important determinant of power. The more alternatives an organization has available relative to its target, the more power it has. Going back to the crude oil situation, it was only when the OPEC countries got together and formed a united bloc in the early 1970s that they succeeded in wresting the power from the oil-consuming countries.

Furthermore, it is the *marginal* impact of an alternative that is important. Consider the situation in the following example.

■ A small soap manufacturer was producing and selling fancy soap to four hundred customers when it was approached by a large chain store and asked to provide soap for the chain under its brand name. At this point, it was operating at 90 percent of capacity, and the contract offered by the store was in the region of 25 percent of capacity. The offer looked good, and the company went ahead and expanded capacity by 30 percent (the smallest feasible expansion for a new plant). After one year of operation with the new plant, the chain store demanded a substantial reduction in its contract price. Despite the fact that the manufacturer had four hundred alternatives, the impact of losing the chain store contract would have been disastrous. Instead of operating at about 90 percent capacity, it would have been operating at about 70 percent capacity, which would have brought it well below break-even with the new fixed cost structure. The soap company had been outmaneuvered in this case, due to the *marginal* impact of the chain store alternative.

Therefore, analysis of the alternative structures should consider the marginal impacts of alternatives. The question to ask is, What difference does my withholding my resources make to the target, and what difference does their withholding their resources have on me?

Leveraging Existing Influence

Often it is possible to leverage existing influence in a situation to achieve a power position.

■ Consider the situation in which a truck seat manufacturer persuaded the truck driver's union to demand installation of his seats in truck bodies. The seat manufacturer did not have the power to get the truck assemblers to do as he wished, so he turned to those people who would gain the greatest benefit from the use of his truck seats. By developing influence with the union, he managed to employ their power to accomplish his goal.

Therefore, in the analysis of situations for the development of a power base, it is often useful to ask what parties *do* have a power base with the target and whether the organization can use influence with them to accomplish what it cannot do on its own. An insightful political analysis identifies not only the relationships that are amenable to direct manipulation but also those that are amenable to indirect manipulation.

Use of Authority

Authority is "legitimized" political capability, that is, legitimized power and influence (Pfeffer 1981). To the extent that an organization allows a person to induce, coerce, persuade, and obligate others, that person has legitimate power and influence and hence legitimate *formal* authority. To the extent that people in the organization who are being induced, coerced, persuaded, and obligated by an individual feel that these actions are legitimate, the individual has legitimate power and influence and hence legitimate *informal* authority. The actual authority of a person in a situation is really his informal authority in the situation. This informal authority can be greater or smaller than the formal authority conferred on the person by the organization.

Why then do we need to have formal authority in an organization? If there were not some kind of ballpark indication of authority within which the members of an organization knew they had to operate, the organization would become paralyzed by people trying to sort out the limits of their authority in the face of counteraction by others. The formal authority attached to various positions in an organization sets boundaries from which individuals cannot move too far without serious resistance from other members of the firm. The larger the organization, the more important it is to have these boundaries.

There are limits to authority, and these limits are broadly set by the organization in a formal sense, yet they are specifically set by each individual in the situation in an informal sense. The informal authority granted to a person in a situation is decided by each other person in the situation, and what may constitute a legitimate action by some may not be regarded as legitimate by others who may feel that the actor is overstepping the mark. One need only look to the protests against the Vietnam War in the 1960s for a visible example of this phenomenon, during which the power and influence of the U.S. government were challenged by people who felt that the government was exceeding its legitimate power and influence, namely, its authority.

Authority in a situation gives rise to opportunities for developing a power base. An individual usually is given authority to accomplish some purpose. The fact that an individual has the authority to do it confers on him a mantle of formal legitimacy that the targets may not have. In such situations, the individual has an edge over anyone who is not regarded as having formal authority.

Have you ever wondered why some people are on so many committees that appear to be extremely boring and tedious? Being on the committee often confers some authority on them. This situation was particularly relevant in an industry committee that was formed to talk with the government on new regulations. Members of the industry were asked to form a committee on regulation, and there was much jockeying by companies that wanted to be selected for the committee. Each company recognized that only a few companies would be represented and that these companies then would have the authority to speak for the industry as a whole.

BUILDING A POWER BASE

Since power is specific to a situation, it is difficult to identify specific bases of power. The source of political capability varies from situation to situation, and we would therefore end up with an immense checklist of little practical value. However, using our previous concepts, it is possible to identify what the source of power in a specific situation is or will be. An industry analysis as outlined by Hofer and Schendel (1978) (a volume in the original West Series in Business Policy and Planning) or by Porter (1980) is an excellent starting tool for identifying potential or emerging sources of power. By anticipating changes in the industry chain from suppliers to distributors to end users, and what bottlenecks will occur in this chain, we can identify potential shortages of scarce, needed, deployable, and convertible resources. Using this idea, MacMillan (1983) has developed a list of opportunities for preempting power positions in the industry chain. These appear in Table 2.2.

As the table illustrates, there are five major areas of opportunity for preempting power situations, and within each area are several possible targets. Each of these is briefly discussed next. However, the reader should be aware that these represent general opportunities only. Actual opportunities will vary within different industries and will change over time as changes occur in technology, market demographics, and the industry life cycle itself. For example, in a stage of rapid growth, the available pressure points will likely lie with preferential access to key suppliers. As an industry matures and supplies have been secured, the pressure points shift more toward the consumer or distribution end of the chain. Real power comes from being able to *anticipate* bottlenecks and *preempt* targets by positioning yourself there first, so that you have the lion's share of the particular resource.

Supply System Opportunities

Critical Raw Materials and Components. Gaining priority access to critical components in a time of high growth in demand can give the organization a major advantage. For instance, Atari was able to take a major video game market share because it had secured supply sources of integrated circuit chips when chips were in short supply. During this time, even a company as large as General Elec-

Table 2.2 Sources of Preemptive Opportunities

Supply Systems
1. Secure access to raw materials or components
2. Preempt production equipment
3. Dominate supply logistics

Product
1. Securing accelerated approval from agencies
2. Securing product development and delivery skills

Production Systems
1. Vertical integration with key suppliers
2. Secure scarce and critical production skills

Customers
1. Building early brand awareness
2. Training customers in usage skills
3. Capturing key accounts

Distribution and Service Systems
1. Occupation of prime locations
2. Preferential access to key distributors
3. Dominance of distribution logistics
4. Access to superior service capabilities
5. Development of distributor skills

tric was seriously hampered in its expansion into microprocessor-based appliances, due to lack of access to computer chip supplies. Note that Atari's position was not permanent. As new chip capacity came on-line and growth in video game sales decelerated, Atari lost its power position because its basis of power—access to scarce supplies—was no longer valid. Note also that supplies need not be physical or exotic. Data services companies have secured enduring niches by locking in critical professional sources or publications or both, denying competitors sufficient remaining sources for the development of viable alternative services.

Production Equipment. When double-knit fabrics were first introduced in the United States, the equipment to produce such fabrics could be secured only from one European supplier. One of the textile producers in the United States was able to preempt a dominant market position by placing sufficient orders with the supplier to tie up this production capacity for eighteen months. Without access to production equipment, their competitors were unable to build production capacity.

Supply System Logistics.   Sometimes all that is needed is priority access to the *means of delivering* the supplies, not to the supplies themselves. A considerable advantage accrued to oil companies who preempted "pipeline space" in the pipelines that pumped crude oil from well sources to refineries in the Northeast—so much so that Justice Department intervention (a risk of such power plays) eventually occurred. In times of boom, first-in-line or priority access to railroad cars or shipping holds creates major advantages for the preemptor of such access, particularly if specialized carriers are needed (such as refrigerated or high-pressure conveyances).

Product Opportunities

Accelerated Approval.   An opportunity for product/service preemption occurs in those highly regulated industries where the product or service requires a regulatory approval process that takes an extended period. Here it may be possible to preempt the market by persuading the agency involved to agree to an accelerated approval program with the regulators, so that the product moves ahead of those of the competition. The first company to secure accelerated approval has virtual exclusivity, since usually the agency logistically cannot handle any more than one acceleration of approval. This happened with anti-ulcer drug therapy products, where one company's product got out of the regulatory pipeline well ahead of others, due to an accelerated approval program.

Product Development Skills.   Another area where preemption is possible is by securing the lion's share of the pool of skills needed to develop a product. For years the degree to which companies were successful in electronics depended on their being "*the* place to work" for the best electronics engineers; the same is now happening in genetic engineering. In particular, the astute strategist may be able to anticipate what key new skills may be needed, and will be in short supply, in the future. For example, it is almost inevitable that commodities businesses are going to be able to preempt positions in many countries that are facing escalating foreign exchange problems if they can secure the dominant share of those few people expert in the structuring of international bartering or countertrading deals.

Production Systems

Vertical Integration.   Being the first company to undertake vertical integration allows the company to acquire, at a good price, the most reliable and lowest-cost suppliers. This move also leaves the competitors at the mercy of higher-cost or less reliable suppliers. Alternatively, it may be appropriate to vertically integrate forward and secure access to the most effective distribution channels.

Production Skills.   Securing the dominant share of critical production skills needed to produce the product, such as die makers, precision machinists, or other skilled workers, has often given particular firms a competitive edge—especially in the construction or military contract business. The next generation of manufacturer/assemblers will probably be those that have cornered the market in engineers and technicians skilled in robotics, and there will be distinct advantages to those foundries that can secure the few engineers that can redesign and manufacture products using modern casting technology.

Customers

Early Usage and Brand Awareness.   It is important to note that with new (or substantially redesigned) products and services, the credibility and acceptance of the product poses a problem, and it may be possible to secure a dominant position by rapidly building brand awareness with, and product acceptance by, opinion-leading initial customers. To accomplish this, it could be highly effective to reduce the "risk of first trial" for these initial customers—particularly if the product is a substitute for an existing product and there is some reluctance to take the risk of switching. For example, by guaranteeing performance, and by agreeing not to bill the customer until the product had been proven, a synthetic cloth company was able to persuade an initial group of influential industrial customers to replace their cotton filter cloth applications with synthetics. With these influential orders in hand, it was easy to convince other customers to place orders. By reducing the risk for the first few purchasing agents, the synthetic cloth producer was able to preempt the business from its other, less aggressive, competitors. The foothold thus created proved to be of lasting benefit. "Reduction of risk" strategies can be particularly powerful for preempting footholds in international markets, where customers may be leery of risking their resources (or their professional reputations) on an untried product from an unknown foreign supplier.

Enhancing Customer Skills. Another area for preemptive opportunities is to identify key skills needed by the customer in order to use or sell the product effectively, and to provide training in those skills. For instance, long before computer programming courses were part of the curriculum for high schools, IBM recognized a need for programming capabilities for its customers, and preempted staunch support on the part of programmers and customers alike with its extensive programming schools. Similar strategies are allowing word processing companies to preempt customer segments by conducting word processing training programs in special areas like law, government agencies, building or government contracting, architecture, consulting, and so on.

Key Accounts. Finally, a major area of opportunity is to identify and secure key accounts, an approach used with success by the first insurance companies that decided to "invade" the group pension fund market and secured the cream of the crop in pension fund accounts; or by Citibank and Chase Manhattan when they moved into international markets and rapidly "occupied" all the major countries before the competition could do so. Access to the few key accounts that account for a large proportion of the business has the additional advantage that competitors must cover larger numbers of smaller accounts to get the same revenue—which can put them at a serious cost disadvantage.

Distribution and Service Systems

Occupation of Prime Locations. To this day, John Deere is acknowledged as having the most effective distribution network in agricultural machinery and occupies the prime locations in American states by having strong distributor representation in the key geographic areas. Sears has been able to occupy prime locations in retailing; McDonald's has built in prime locations for fast food; and Holiday Inn has occupied prime locations in accommodation.

Access to Key Distributors. A second opportunity is to preempt exclusive or dominant access to key distributors. Particular attention must be given to opportunities to preempt *new* distributors. Coca-Cola's aggressive moves into the *major* fast food chains (like McDonald's) secured for them a lasting niche in this new distribution channel, while BIC (ball-pens) and L'eggs (pantyhose) preempted the originally "nontraditional" supermarket chains for a long-term advantage. The efficacy of such preemptive moves into new distribution channels is particularly enhanced by the fact that the competitors are often hamstrung from following suit by their own powerful *existing* distributors.

Priority Position in Distribution Logistics.   Opportunities may lie in preempting the distribution *logistics*. By building a huge modern infrastructure of grain terminals with unit train loading and off-loading facilities in key locations, and specialized fleets of railroad cars and export vessels, Cargill was able to forge a position as one of the five dominant grain dealers in the world. AT&T was able for decades to dominate the long-distance call market with its long-lines network. The major soft drink producers were able to secure equally long-lasting niches by preemptive licensing of local bottlers. Major perishable food manufacturers like Pillsbury preempted prime retail space by installation of freezers and coolers.

Service Systems.   Another powerful source of preemptive opportunities lies in the area of service. Particularly in the United States, where labor costs of skilled workers are very high, radically different service challenges are emerging. To name but one: Demographic trends toward families in which both partners work are creating new opportunities for packaging major appliance offerings that stress high reliability, utilizing diagnostics from installed microprocessors to minimize service needs. This opportunity could preempt important niches in the major appliance business. Sears is currently experimenting with the one-stop servicing of *all* appliances in a home with each visit, which could preempt a niche for that growing segment of families where nobody is at home during normal working hours.

Enhancing Needed Distributor Skills.   A fifth opportunity lies in identifying key existing or emerging skill requirements among distributors, and preempting distributor loyalty by providing such skills. Many a supplier has carved a relatively long-lived niche in the market by offering services such as inventory or merchandising services, or training schools to train managers and employees of these distributors. In a similar vein, First Bank of Minneapolis geared up for interstate banking by securing many of the best regional banks as franchises of its First Interstate System—which provided complex software systems and support skills that regionals needed to operate a modern bank.

The preemption potential of the industry chain is somewhat easier to describe than are the sources of power available *within* the organization. Again, the reader is referred to the literature on personal power for such discussions.

A power play may not be appropriate in all situations. Some occasions are better met with the use of influence.

SOURCES OF INFLUENCE

With influence we are concerned with the ways a player may change the perceptions of the targets rather than changing the situation. To change perceptions, the influencer must undertake a successful communication process, so certain resources must be at her disposal. First, the actor must be able to communicate with the influencees, which means that an appropriate communication system is needed. Second, the influencees must be prepared to accept the communication. Third, they must believe the communication, so the influencer must have a sound knowledge of the beliefs and value systems of the influencees. Fourth, the influencer must communicate information that is relevant to the situation and to the influencees. Fifth, the influence depends upon the sets of past commitments that the influencees have made as well as the strength of these commitments. These five requirements determine the kinds of resources that are necessary for the exercise of influence in any situation.

The strategies for building an influence base focus on a complementary set of factors addressed in building a power base: strategic influence resources, control of alternatives, power, and authority. In a business situation, the first issue is to decide who the key decision makers are in the target group or organization, for the perceptions of these key decision makers will shape the targets' decisions and actions. First identify the key decision makers, and then start to build your influence strategy using the building blocks that follow.

Strategic Influence Resources

It is convenient to categorize these resources into three broad classes of strategic influence resources: audience, information, and commitments.

Establishing Audience.   Audience is the extent to which the influencer can physically communicate with the influencees; the rapport that he can establish with them on the basis of knowledge of their values; and their propensity for receiving and paying attention to the influence effort, based on their perception of his prestige, credibility, reliability, and expertise. This means that the influencer needs to develop a communication system and some credibility with the target influencees, and pull together information that will get them to readjust their thinking in favor of what the influencer wants.

Development of communication systems and credibility structures and generating a thorough knowledge of the value system of the targets can prove costly. Furthermore, the resources deployed to develop audience must often be diverted from other purposes, such as development of a power base. Where attention in the literature is given to development of audience, it is generally in such areas as marketing and public relations, and it tends to ignore the need for developing audience with other important strategic stakeholders, such as banks, shareholders, government officials, competitors, and so on. As a result, inadequate attention is given to creating effective communication systems, pools of knowledge, and the necessary credibility with these stakeholders.

■ Perhaps the most glaring example of this is reported by Lederer and Burdick (1958) (in their factual epilogue to the book). Apparently, the United States once donated a huge consignment of tractors to Pakistan. Within days it was commonly accepted in the countryside that Russia had sent the tractors. Local Communists had broken into the storage area one night and stenciled a red hammer and sickle on every flat surface of every tractor! All the audience and credibility that went with the large economic investment were captured for the cost of a few cans of red paint (and the creative application of the concepts of influence we are discussing here). The Communists got a credible and comprehensible message across, with a simple communication system, to the target audience.

■ Another example is found in the case of an insurance company that spent a great deal of effort attempting to attract stockholders with massive public relations and advertising efforts on radio, television, and in the press. Then, analysis revealed that over 70 percent of its stocks were held by institutions (such as pension funds and churches). A substantial proportion of the funds it was deploying to the mass media could have been far more effectively deployed in developing small teams of people geared specifically to cultivating the key decision makers among such investor groups. Once this was recognized and implemented, substantial improvements in results were obtained, at about one-half the expenditure.

Possession of Strategic Information.   As Pettigrew (1973), among others, points out, the second type of resource that is required for effective influence is information that is strategically relevant to the influence attempt. This is the key information that is required if changes in the perception of the influencee are to be accomplished.

■ For instance, while our current influence attempt may be moderately successful (you have read this far!), if we changed the nature of the information we are bringing you and began to discuss food consumption patterns in a medieval monastery, we would lose the attention of many who have stuck with us so far. The kind of information we would be bringing to bear on your perceptions would not be seen as relevant either to your value systems or to the influence attempt we are supposed to be making, which is to restructure your perceptions of strategy.

Developing information that is relevant to the situation requires analysis and insight, just as in the case of audience. A trade-off must be made not only between resources that are to be deployed to developing a power base or to developing an influence base, but also within the influence strategy between resources deployed to developing audience and resources deployed to developing strategic information via intelligence systems. These systems keep in touch with the value systems and strategic information necessary to maintain the interest and attention of the influencees.

Commitments.   The final general resource that is important in an influence system is commitment. People commit themselves in two ways: to principles and to other people. For instance, business people may be committed to principles relating to the value system they hold (such as not doing business with foreign countries that espouse certain political beliefs) or to ways of conducting business (such as never giving discounts, never accepting under-the-counter deals, and so on). Alternatively, they may be committed to people in the form of formal or informal agreements. The commitment of Japanese employers to providing lifetime job security to employees is an example. A commitment to fulfill a certain contract is another example.

Commitments can be regarded as voluntary reductions of alternatives. By committing themselves, either to principles or to people, actors automatically reduce the alternative courses of action available to them.

The extent to which the targets have commitments has an important effect on the success of the influence attempt. In the first place, the commitment structure of the targets is the fundamental process whereby the influencer can activate their sense of obligation. If she can argue successfully that a course of action contemplated by them is in conflict with their commitments, then she has a chance of succeeding in preventing them from carrying out that action. Second, if she can somehow get the targets committed to herself, the ability to prevent an action that is unsuitable to her is further enhanced.

■ An example in which the structure of commitments played a key role in the influence process occurred in the 1970s, when many companies were faced with the Arab blacklisting of organizations doing business with Israel. Many companies that wanted Arab-world business were forced to forgo this business because they felt obliged to honor their existing commitments to Israel.

Therefore, a careful analysis of the structure of commitments is an important prerequisite for the effectiveness of an influence play, and it may be vital to deploy resources toward developing commitments of key actors in the situation before any move is made.

It is important to recognize that influence resources, like power resources, are considered strategic only when they are deployable in the situation, and when it takes time and effort to acquire them.

Control of Alternatives as a Basis of Influence

As in the case of power, the extent to which the alternatives available in an influence system can be controlled is a major determinant of the influence base. If an organization or an individual is the only actor that has an effective communications system, or credibility, or the strategic information necessary for the influencees, it will monopolize the influence process. To the extent that its targets also have communication systems or credibility, however, its influence is reduced. Moreover, its targets' commitment structures are also of relevance. To the extent that they are committed to principles or people, they reduce their own alternatives.

- A large travel company publically committed itself to a policy of guaranteeing to undercut the lowest prices in the market, to put pressure on a smaller competitor. The smaller competitor responded by drastically cutting prices in their competitor's key sales area. Traditional customers of the larger company went to it, demanding that the price of the smaller company be undercut. The smaller company had fewer inquiries in that area, and the people making inquiries were told that it was "a good time to take up the larger company's offer." As a result, the larger company was compelled to send many tours out considerably below cost, and in trying to economize disaffected a substantial proportion of its customers.

- At one stage, a large number of companies in the textile industry were on the verge of collapse or had collapsed. One member of the industry was a private company that was in fairly sound shape but was being encumbered by the image of the industry as a whole. Suppliers were loath to supply, investors' confidence was low, and customers were expressing concern that the orders they placed would not be delivered. The chairman of the sound company decided that he would have to differentiate the company from others in the industry if his company were to have credibility. When the next company in the industry went into voluntary liquidation, he made a publically announced bid for the failing company. If his bid had been accepted, he would have been able to resell at a modest profit. The offer was not accepted, but the fact that the offer was made boosted confidence in his company within days, and, for a considerable period after that, he had no trouble with suppliers or customers, most of whom were keen to do business with him *rather than anyone else*, because he had established a unique credibility in the industry. Interestingly enough, this was accomplished at absolutely no cost to his company.

These examples were intended to demonstrate some of the facets of the control of influence resources. A careful analysis of the structure of such alternatives is often difficult because of the intangibility of factors such as degree of commitment and level of credibility, but this difficulty should enhance, rather than detract from, the need to take them specifically into consideration before a strategic move is launched.

Leveraging a Power Position to Secure Influence

Influence can also be obtained by the use of power, using an indirect approach. If a person (or an organization) does not have influence with a target but has power over another party who *does* have influence, it may be possible to get the third party to exert influence. This is particularly important in situations in which the person to be influenced steadfastly rejects any attempts or overtures at persuasion or obligation on the part of the influencer. In these situations, the necessary audience is absent and the influence seeker is compelled to turn to parties who do have audience.

■ In the United States, some companies have commissioned reputable public opinion surveyors to test the public sentiment on issues involving regulation, particularly if these issues appeared to be spearheaded by a vociferous and well-organized but minor interest group. These companies knew that there is no way that they themselves can credibly argue that the majority of the population disagree; the company's self-interest when making this claim is too evident. Hence, they "buy" the credibility of reputable pollsters.

Use of Authority

The same arguments that applied to the use of authority in building a power base apply here, since authority is legitimized power *and* influence. The subtleties of the difference, however, can best be explained by an example.

■ The very fact that you are reading this book means that some kind of authority has been conferred on us, even though we have never met. The major component of our authority is influence rather than power. We are trying to change your perceptions of the world in which you live. To the extent that you have been *required* to read this book, we have formal authority. To the extent that we can persuade you in the opening chapters that the book is worth reading, we start developing informal authority. If we asked you to turn now to page 100 and read it before continuing here, many of you probably would be prepared to do it. You would feel we have a legitimate right to get you to do this. If, however, we asked you to go out and purchase a certain brand of toothpaste, few of you would feel that we have a right to influence you in this way. We would have overstepped the informal authority you grant us.

SUMMARY: KEY CONCEPTS

In this chapter, a number of simplifications are made. No attention is given to the capability of people to recognize their power and influence in a situation, nor is their adeptness at exercising their political capability. The discussion is carried out as if persuasion, inducement, and coercion could be carried out in a pure form, when a mix of these means of manipulation is usually used in practice.

Manipulation is discussed as if it were a unilateral action on the part of the manipulator, when the target may be making counter-moves and when the target and the manipulator could be negotiating a joint agreement while the manipulative action is taking place. To take a simple case, a manipulator may negotiate with his target the size of the inducement to be given for the manipulator to be successful. It is only for conceptual convenience that the process of manipulation is discussed as if it were separate from other types of political action.

1. Power can be conceived of as the capacity of an actor to restructure the situation so that her targets will act as she desires.

2. Influence can be conceived of as the capacity of an actor to restructure the targets' perceptions of situations, so that they will act as he desires.

3. Strategic power resources, control of alternatives, influence, and authority are major bases of power in a situation.

4. Strategic influence resources, control of alternatives, power, and authority are major bases of influence in a situation.

5. Both power and influence are situationally determined; that is, having power and influence in one situation does not necessarily mean having power and influence in another.

6. Effective political strategies can be evolved only from a careful analysis of the power and influence potential of the situation. In this case, difficult trade-offs must be made between deployment of resources to develop power or influence (or both) in the situation.

3

Negotiation

In the previous chapter, we assured that the strategist could unilaterally get others to act in the way the strategist desired by manipulating them. Oftentimes such results are not possible, and the strategist must negotiate with the targets.

By negotiation, we mean a situation in which two or more actors whose interests are in conflict attempt to come to some kind of joint agreement about how they will behave with respect to one another. The important fundamental concepts of negotiation have been extremely well explored by various authors. In this chapter, a great deal of the argument is based on a few key works by Schelling (1963), Kennedy (1965), Walton and McKersie (1969), Karass (1970), Cohen (1980), and Fisher and Ury (1981). There is no hope of being able to cover these works in a single chapter; the reader is strongly encouraged to explore the concepts further, starting with these references.

THE CONCEPT OF NEGOTIATION

To introduce the concepts of negotiation, let us take a simple case of a person called Seller, who wishes to sell a small business. Karass (1970) points out that there appear to be two definitive limits to the kind of deal that Seller might make. First, there is a lower limit below which Seller will not sell the business at all. This is Seller's *bargaining base*. If seller gets an offer anywhere below this base, the deal is impossible. Second, there is a less obvious but important upper limit that Seller feels will be the best possible price she can hope to get. This is Seller's *aspiration base*, which Seller does not really expect to

Figure 3.1 Seller's Aspiration and Bargaining Bases

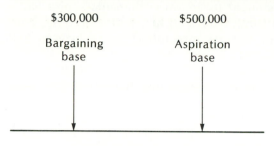

$300,000 $500,000

Bargaining base   Aspiration base

have exceeded under even the best circumstances. Suppose Seller's aspiration base and bargaining base are as depicted in Figure 3.1.

Then suppose that Seller decided to place an advertisement offering her business for sale in the local newspaper. If you were Seller, what price would you ask for the business? In most Western societies, people are inclined to put up an initial offer on or above the aspiration base with the expectation that they will have to move down. (This is not necessarily true in other societies, however.)

For the sake of simplicity, let us suppose that Seller's initial offer is at her aspiration base, and the business goes on the market at $500,000. Suppose then that a person called Buyer is interested in the business. He, too, will have an aspiration base, in his case the lowest price that he thinks he will be able to pay for the business, and a bargaining base, in this case the highest price he is prepared to pay for the business. These bases are as depicted in Figure 3.2.

Figure 3.2 Buyer's Aspiration and Bargaining Bases

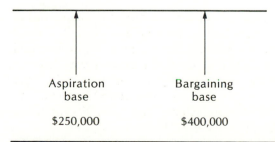

Aspiration base   Bargaining base

$250,000 $400,000

If Buyer follows the expected pattern, he will make an initial offer that is equal to or lower than his aspiration base. Let us suppose that his first offer is at his aspiration base. If we put the two figures together (always remembering that neither Seller nor Buyer knows their target's bases), then we get Figure 3.3.

Immediately, we can see several things from Figure 3.3. First, unless the two bargaining bases overlap to form a contract zone, there can be no deal. If a deal is going to be struck, it will be somewhere in the contract zone between $300,000 and $400,000. Second, if Seller's initial price is $500,000 and Buyer's initial offer is $250,000, then obviously one of them must make a concession if a deal is going to go through at all. Schelling (1963) argues that neither will make a concession as long as they both think the other might make a concession. If this is correct, then some interesting implications emerge. If Seller cannot find some way of "locking" herself onto the $500,000 offer and Buyer *can* lock himself onto the $250,000 offer, then unless Seller has an alternative buyer, she will find that she *has* to make some kind of a concession or the negotiation will deadlock.

The reverse applies to Buyer. Therefore, both parties have to find a lock; but the problem is that if they *both* do, then neither can move. The one who cannot find a lock will find him- or herself being inexorably pulled to his or her bargaining base. We shall explore this problem next, after discussing some functions that shape the basic nature of negotiating situations.

Figure 3.3 Buyer and Seller Combined

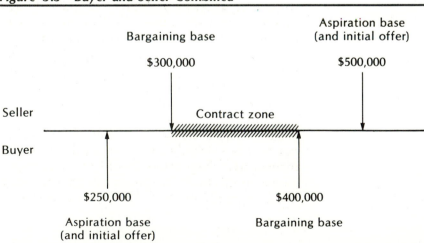

Figure 3.4   Negotiation Strategies as a
Function of the Basic Negotiating Situation

Distributive (win–lose) negotiations	Integrative (win–win) negotiations

One-time negotiation | Repeated negotiations
One issue | Multiple issues
Immediate execution of deal | Delayed execution of deal

Basic Nature of the Negotiation Situations

The example just presented is a simple one: a one-time negotiation between two parties with one issue (price) and immediate execution of the deal. This is a good example of what is called a *distributive negotiation* (Walton and McKersie 1969). Each party attempts to win, to take the "largest share of the pie." In popular parlance, this is a win-lose situation. In simple situations, particularly one-time deals in which the execution of the deal takes place immediately after the agreement, a negotiating strategy that takes a win-lose approach may be the most appropriate. Typical examples are the sale of used equipment or sale of property.

However, much of the current literature suggests that as the complexity increases and there is a need for the parties to maintain a long-term relationship, or as the time delay between striking the deal and executing it increases, negotiation strategy must shift to a win-win approach in which both parties feel they are better off as a result of the deal and are eager to make sure the execution goes smoothly. Bargaining with suppliers, labor unions, customers, and sometimes even competitors, where there are repeated deals or long-term contracts, suggests win-win tactics. Figure 3.4 portrays the negotiation strategy continuum and identifies the factors that drive the situation from a win-lose to a win-win situation.

This chapter focuses primarily on the case of win-win negotiations, not because distributive negotiation is not important but because distributive negotiations have less application for the processes discussed in this book. The integrative bargaining process is the one that is allied most closely to the political perspective we are exploring.

Negotiating Tactics

Let us first provide some grounding in three basic negotiating tactics:

1. the bluff
2. the threat
3. the promise

(The material in this section is based largely on the work of Schelling 1963).

THE BLUFF

Each negotiator must try to bluff that his current offer is his last offer. For this bluff to succeed, each must find a way of committing himself to his bluff. In the previous example, unless Seller can *commit* herself in some way to her offer of $500,000, Buyer will drag Seller's price down. Thus, bluff tactics involve developing a set of commitments to each offer that attempts to persuade the target that this offer is the final one. What we need to consider are the nature and implications of these commitments.

In the first place, Seller needs to be aware that Buyer is also committing himself to his bluffs. If the deal looks good and Seller has committed herself too firmly to the current offer, and it appears that Buyer has committed himself completely to his offer, then they may find themselves in deadlock, even though a very acceptable deal could be made.

Therefore, it is important in formulating the bluff to make sure that you have a loophole by which you can get out of the commitment, if necessary. If you have this loophole, then you can allow your target to talk you out of the commitment, or you can even talk yourself out of it. The commitment is not a simple case of formulating some unequivocal reason why you cannot budge and then sticking to it.

What usually happens, then, is that both parties formulate commitments to their current offers, bluffing that these are their last offers, and then they try to persuade their targets that the other's commitment is not final. When one party is convinced that the target will not concede, she allows herself to be talked out of her current commitment and makes a new offer. Typically, but not necessarily, what also happens is that targets start with moderately low commitments and these increase as they move toward their bargaining base.

However, a real danger arises if they both increase their commitments as they get closer to their bargaining bases, because there is the peculiar situation that the closer they get to an increasingly desirable deal for both, the greater the danger of deadlock. At times like this, there is a great pressure to release the tension and accept the target's offer, at the other party's expense.

Having discussed the nature of bluffing, it is perhaps useful to consider some of the tactics that can be employed in bluffing. Schelling (1963) has identified a number of such tactics, which are summarized in Table 3.1. *Bluffs basically involve formulating a commitment to a current offer, with a nonobvious loophoole that allows you to release yourself from this commitment if you have to do so.*

Before discussing the specific tactics involved in executing a bluff, we wish to make some general observations about the nature of *all* tactics.

Tactics are not risk-free. With every tactic discussed next, greater reward is sought but *by increasing the risk* of deadlock. The risk-free move is to accept the target's most recent offer, but this is costly. The highest potential reward comes from sticking firmly to one's initial offer, but then one runs the risk of having the deal deadlock or fall through. With every tactic, the negotiator has to trade off the reward he wants to shoot for, against the risk of having the deal fall through.

Table 3.1   Bluff Tactics

- Commitment to a deadline
- Commitment to a third party
- Use of a lackey
- Use of an agent
- Commitment to the public
- Commitment to principle/policy
- Commitment to a precedent
- Commitment to a target via a third party
- Commitment via obstinacy
- Invoking an alternative
- Playing for time

The second thing to note about tactics is that they *are* only tactics; they are a single play in a more complex strategy in which a number of tactics are employed to fit the overall direction the negotiator wishes to take. The target (opponent) can anticipate tactics that are used too often, and so can develop countertactics. Also, successfully using the same tactic with the same people too frequently causes the target to become emotionally upset and act irrationally in the haste to "get even," even if it means the deal has to fall through. Then win-lose dynamics emerge. Using a mix of tactics in negotiations is therefore appropriate.

Commitment to a Deadline

■ A property seller sent a signed contract by messenger to a potential client with a letter containing the following message: "I have decided that $500,000 is the lowest offer I can possibly accept. I am enclosing a contract to that effect because, unfortunately, I am leaving for Chicago on urgent business. I am very sorry, but the contract states that if you haven't signed it by 5:00 p.m. today, I'll have to consider the deal off. There is nothing more I can do; I have just run out of time. I hope it works out." (The contract was signed by the buyer.)

If this tactic works, how does it work? Basically, the property dealer in this situation made a final offer and committed herself by setting a deadline and finding ways of avoiding communication until the deadline had passed. If the deal looks good to the target and the deadline looks realistic, then the target has no alternative but to accept the offer. Initiative is in the hands of the person setting the deadline.

Commitment to a Third Party

The essence of the next tactic is the negotiator's seeming commitment to a third party, so that he runs the risk of punishment if he does not stick to his offer. Then, it is not his fault that he is being so obstinate!

■ The boss of a small company was faced with the problem of a valuable supplier (to whom the company was a valuable customer) who every year demanded at least a 10 percent increase in material prices. One year, the boss went to his board and asked them for a directive demanding that he not accept any price increases "due to the profit erosionary impact of inflation." He used this document to persuade his target that it was only at risk to his position that he could give the supplier a 3 percent increase. (The two parted on good terms.)

Use of a Lackey

■ The chief of a data processing service company used to send out her salespeople with explicit and demanding instructions when they were closing data processing contracts with clients. They were given written instructions as to what prices, guarantees, and terms to meet. Whenever the client made a demand, the salesperson would check the instructions and indicate whether the demand fitted the instructions. If the client continued to demand, the salesperson would promise to return after checking with the boss. On return, a slightly modified position would be presented. On the relatively few occasions when the salesperson was dismissed by the client, then and only then would the boss take over the negotiations.

This tactic is very important. In the first place, the boss may have too much authority. After all, the boss is the boss and can be subjected to demands from a target that would be unthinkable to demand from a subordinate. Thus, using a lackey is a way of restricting authority to make concessions. Second, it sets out the ballpark in which the game will be played. Before the main protagonists get together, they must make sure that they have, to some extent, signaled ahead of time some limits on the concessions that will be demanded of them. Third, it is a way of softening up the target. Fourth, it provides an opportunity of seeing how tough-minded the target is, and allows the negotiator to assess the target's strengths and weaknesses before she exposes herself.

Use of an Agent

Instead of negotiating himself, the strategist might employ a professional negotiator to act for him. However, care must be taken that these agents are rewarded in such a way that the reward they receive is commensurate with how well they do for the strategist, and not just for closing the deal. Many professional negotiators are rewarded just for closing the deal. By providing the right incentives, getting them to focus on driving a good deal is possible.

Use of an agent is important because the agent can be given instructions, like the lackey; but freed from the emotion and tension involved, the agent is less inclined to accept a target's early offer in the haste to get the deal settled.

Public Commitment of Reputation

If one can find a way of communicating a bluff to an interested audience, one is committed to keeping it.

■ Prior to a round of labor contract negotiations, union leaders announced to the press that they were going to get at least a fifty-cent-per-hour increase for their members. When the negotiations got under way, they could argue convincingly that their reputation and credibility with the membership would be destroyed if they accepted any less.

The major point about bluff tactics is that they should be convincing. The union's targets were placed in the awkward position of finding ways (via concessions on other issues) of making any concession by the union on wages look less damaging to the leaders' reputations.

Commitment to Principle/Policy

■ A chemical company uses the following argument in negotiations with customers: "It is 'against our policy' to give discounts for large volume. This would give the larger companies a competitive edge over their smaller competitors, who have supported us for many years." Since the company's products are of high quality, they are able to get away with this commitment.

Commitment to policy or principles are rather easy to invoke and have the advantage that they are extremely difficult to subvert. If someone tries to attack a commitment to a principle, the implications are that the principles are in doubt! If someone tries to attack a commitment to policy, one finds it difficult to get back to the amorphous "source" of that policy.

Commitment to Precedent

A common argument in labor negotiations is that if we concede this year, we will have to concede next year as well. Since a concession would set a precedent for later negotiations, we cannot afford to set that precedent. (Then, it is up to the target to persuade us that this is not the case.)

■ A manufacturer of quality chrome tube furniture refuses to make special orders on the argument that if she makes special orders for one, she will have to make it for all the other customers, and this would drive her costs up.

If we can argue convincingly that a concession sets a precedent for negotiations over time and across many targets, we have a strong argument for not conceding.

Commitment to a Target Via a Third Party

If the situation can be structured in such a way that we can "commit" ourselves to our target in the face of conflict with a third party, then the third party bears the brunt of the blame for being unyielding and unreasonable, while we appear to be sympathetic and rational.

■ A chemical company was trying to license a new product from an overseas patent holder. The patent holding company sent two negotiators, one of whom was particularly obstinate, unreasonable, and obnoxious. Some time after the negotiations were started, the obnoxious person was "called away," and the second member of the team persuaded the representatives of the chemical company that if they could come to a quick settlement just below what his unconceding colleague was demanding, he could get his colleague to accept it.

Commitment Via Obstinacy

It is possible that by the force of sheer obstinacy (feigned or not), we could convince the targets that whatever their arguments, we are not going to move from our offer. (This approach can be risky—we could make the targets angry and they might refuse to continue the negotiation. They might also become unwilling to negotiate with us in the future.)

Invoking an Alternative

A common method of commitment is to claim that we have an alternative offer.

■ An antique dealer would try to arrange for one of the potential purchasers to call her while she was meeting with another client interested in the same piece. This was a convincing demonstration by the antique dealer that more than one alternative was available.

Playing for Time

As a counter to a target's commitment, when the negotiator does not have a ready commitment for his bluff, there are a variety of ways of playing for time.

Postponement. Finding a plausible way of postponing further negotiation is a useful ploy which should be prepared beforehand so that one does not have to use a spurious reason to break off discussion.

Feigning Misunderstanding. If we are somehow unable to understand a target's arguments, we can buy time.

■ On one occasion, an executive who was faced with a demand for rate increases in the travel industry calculated the cost structure five times, each time getting a different answer. She then said that perhaps she had better sit down with her accountant and work things out. This gave her time to develop a countertactic.

Raising Another Issue. Since few negotiations are about a single issue, such as price, it is often possible to turn to another issue and argue that while playing for time on the current issue. (This tactic is a favorite ploy of politicians who are in a corner.)

Nit-picking. It is sometimes possible to start picking apart the precise nature of the target's bluff, trying to raise a dust cloud over minor points while the major point is being obscured (a tactic favored by many attorneys).

Many more tactics can be employed, but most of the main ones have been covered. Let us therefore turn to the next type of tactical movement: the threat.

THE THREAT

■ After it had installed the extra capacity to support the contract with the chain store, the soap company described in Chapter 2 was faced with the following demand when the contract was to be renegotiated: "We want a reduction of 15 percent in price, or we will take our business to your competitor."

■ A small toy-manufacturing company was operating on a fairly heavy bank overdraft when a credit squeeze took place in the economy. Banks started calling for reductions in overdrafts. After several demands from the bank, the owner of the small company went to the bank manager with the following statement: "In six months, my cash flows will turn around as I hit my seasonal selling peaks. Until then, I will have to continue my overdraft. I will not reduce it; I have inventory to build up. Either leave me alone for six months or foreclose on me. My way you get your money back in full. If you foreclose, you will get about sixty cents on the dollar. I'm really sorry, but you'll have to take it or leave it." (The bank left him alone and put pressure on *other* companies.)

What is happening here? In each case, a threat is involved. The threatener demands certain actions on the part of the target and lays out the conditions that will prevail if that action is not followed. Yet, the threats are different. The chain store stood to lose by being inconvenienced by a disruption of supply while new sources were set up, but they stood to lose far less than the soap manufacturer. This is an example of a *strong* threat: Both parties lose, but the one that makes the threat loses less.

In the case of the toy manufacturer, both parties stood to lose, but the threatener stood to lose much more—his business would be closed down. This is a weak threat—the threatener stands to lose more than the target.

A situation in which the aggressor does not get hurt at all we would not regard as a threat. It would be coercion, "making an offer that cannot be refused."

The problem with a weak threat is that it is often hard to believe that the threatener will actually carry out the threat, since her action would be irrational. Thus, weak threats are suspect and tend to be ignored by most negotiators.

However, let us explore the nature and purpose of the threat a little more clearly. What is the purpose of the threat? It is to get targets to do something they would rather not do. Is the threat made to be successful or to fail? Negotiators do not make threats that they expect to fail. Then, if one formulates a successful threat, does one get hurt? No, because there is no need to carry out the action that would have hurt. The target has behaved as was desired and there is no need for punitive action at all! Who would be hurt more, then, becomes academic—*neither* is hurt.

The weak threat, as well as the strong threat, is a viable tactic, *provided that the negotiator can convince his target that he is prepared to carry out the threat, or better yet, that the threat will be carried out beyond the control of the threatener.*

The negotiator persuades his target that he intends to carry out the threat by *committing* himself to carrying it out. A threat, then, is nothing other than a conditional bluff. In formulating threats, we are back to the whole problem of commitment again. The same type of tactics that we discussed under bluffs applies, and the same problem of finding a loophole applies. In the case of the threat, however, the loophole is even more critical. Particularly with the weak threat, it is important to recognize that our targets know that if we stop to act rationally when they have transgressed, we will not carry out the threat. Therefore, the threat must be carefully spelled out to indicate exactly what the transgressive act is. (If it is not clear, then while we are deciding whether the target has transgressed, we have time to rationalize not executing the threat.) Also important is that the threatener does not allow the targets to spot a loophole, or they will transgress and provide the loophole for the threatener. A good threat would appear to the target to be one that is automatically carried out, and the decision to carry out the threat should appear to be out of the threatener's hands completely.

> ■ The head of a travel company chartering planes during the 1973 oil crisis decided that the arbitrary price increases being announced by the airlines from which he was chartering had to be slowed down. When the next price increase was about to be announced, he wrote to them stating that the proposed 10 percent increase was too high and that unless the airline held it at 5 percent, he would have to cancel all the tours he had arranged for the next year. He further stated that since he would have to be away when the contract was due to be signed, he was signing and forwarding a contract to the airline. If they were not prepared to accept it, they were to notify his administrative manager, who had received instructions to then cancel all tours associated with the airline in question. The head of the travel company would not be available for further discussions, since he was about to depart for a series of highly confidential negotiations in the Far East and Africa.

By structuring the threat so that execution appeared to be automatic, he removed all opportunity for the use of his own discretion should the airline transgress. As a matter of interest, we see many of the elements of the bluff tactics that were discussed before. In this case, there was a deadline, and the head of the travel company found a way of committing himself to the bluff via a lackey (his administrative manager) and of communicating his commitment and the breaking off of communication until the deadline passed. It was also a weak threat, because the damage to his business would have been greater than the loss of his business to the airline. However, from the point of view of the airline, his business was important, or the threat would never have worked. He succeeded in putting the brakes on the automatic price increase pattern that had started to emerge.

Finally, while it appeared to the targets that the threat would automatically be carried out, this was not the case. If the airline had transgressed, the loophole that had been planned involved the lackey frantically calling the head of the airline to say that he had been instructed to cancel all tours and then being "persuaded" to hold off until the boss returned. The boss upon returning would call the airline and demand to know why his subordinate had been "subverted," and he would thus reopen the channels of communication and the negotiations would proceed.

From this example, it is important to recognize the urgent need, once the threat has not succeeded, for both parties to find some way of avoiding the execution of the threat. Thus, the commitment to a threat is much more tricky then the commitment to a bluff. It must appear that the threat is going to be carried out, yet there must be a credible loophole that will put off the execution of the threat. Otherwise, the threatener might find himself firmly committed to doing something that is harmful to himself.

In addition to bluffs and threats, there is still one more negotiating tactic of great importance to be discussed before we turn our attention to negotiating strategy: the promise.

THE PROMISE

■ Every now and then, the airlines agree to some kind of no-frills fare structure whereby the passengers are loaded into the plane and transported to their destinations without fancy meals, movies, and so on. Then, inexorably, one after the other, the frills are reintroduced and the costs skyrocket again. Why should this happen?

■ A large number of companies used to spew thousands of tons of effluents into the Great Lakes. Everyone deplored the impact on the environment, yet no one did anything about it. It took punitive federal laws to slow the pollution. Why was such the case?

Both of these situations (and many other situations that require an agreement between competitors) require a promise. A promise is required in a situation in which joint agreement is necessary for the good of all participants, but if one participant does not cooperate or agrees to cooperate and then cheats, then this participant gains an advantage over the others. (Technically, this sort of situation is known as a Prisoner's Dilemma.)

If the airlines all agree to no-frills flights, but one gives a meal or a movie and the passengers go to them, then all end up giving meals and movies and so on. If one industry decides not to pollute, it makes little difference to the Great Lakes, so everyone pollutes because no one can get everyone not to do so. In both these situations, everyone loses out, because they cannot promise one another not to cheat.

Basically, to create a successful promise, the participants have to find ways of committing themselves to a course of action even when there is an incentive to cheat. Yet, the more everyone is persuaded that the others will not cheat, the greater the incentive for them to cheat. Using this reasoning about others, all targets rationalize that they may as well cheat, so everyone loses. For a promise to be effective, then, certain conditions must be met. First, it must be possible to monitor cheaters; that is to say, a system of checking and catching cheaters must be available. Second, it must be possible to punish cheaters, for, if they cannot be punished, they will cheat anyway. This means that in the absence of a monitoring system or some kind of legal or pseudolegal system for punishing cheaters, the promise is unlikely to succeed.

- Several companies were trying to form a price cartel (in a part of the world where cartels are not illegal), but could not do so because every time price agreements were made, the companies would go out and make under-the-counter price deals with the customers. The cartel stabilized only when the companies came to agreement on a market share arrangement. Each company agreed to a certain market share. A market research organization was employed to determine market share each month, and if one company sold more than its share, it was required to pay a penalty that was used to refund those who sold less than the agreed market share. A means had thus been found both to monitor and to punish cheaters. In this case, a pseudolegal system had to be set up.

- In the case of the companies polluting Lake Michigan, the dilemma they faced was resolved only when a superordinate body (the government) intervened to monitor and punish cheaters by taking legal action against offenders. In this case, a legal system was set up.

Hence, in a situation in which a promise is required, creative attention should be focused on how to develop the requisite monitoring and sanctioning systems. Without them, it is fairly certain that everyone will end up losing.

Signaling Commitment

No matter what the negotiating tactic—bluff, promise, or threat—if the target is not convinced of the negotiator's willingness to follow through, the tactic misses its objective. To be successful, the tactic must signal commitment on the part of the negotiator. Such signaling contains five elements:

1. Finality—the degree to which finality is signaled
2. Specificity—exactly what is desired
3. Alternatives—whether and what alternative options exist for the negotiator
4. Consequences—whether specific action will be taken if the offer is not accepted

5. Control—the degree of control the negotiator still has over the outcome (often expressed in the use of pronouns)

Contrast the following two statements made by a negotiator seeking performance guarantees in an oil recovery plant construction negotiation.

1. If you cannot see your way clear to guaranteeing a high extraction efficiency, I am obliged to start looking at offers from other competitors.
2. *We* must have *95 percent* extraction efficiency. If you can't *guarantee* it, *we* shall have to *take the contract to XYZ, your competitor.*

All four elements are contained in the last statement. The target (in this place, a contractor) has little room for doubt about the negotiator's commitment. What the target *does not* know is whether or not this is a bluff. It little matters. If she is sure of the commitment to action, she is left with the decision, based on her own needs, of conceding to the demand or living with the consequences.

The negotiating tactics we previously discussed are essential for ensuring that the negotiator secures a satisfactory position for himself on those issues that are important to him. It is via a critical few bluffs, threats, and promises that the negotiator takes control of, and assures success in, securing his high-priority needs in even the most collaborative negotiations.

NEGOTIATION STRATEGY

Having discussed the tactics, let us now look at the negotiating strategy. Since most business negotiations involve multiple issues and there are long delays between striking the deal and executing the deal, or the negotiations with the targets are repeated over time, we focus primarily on win-win situations. Examples are negotiations with supplies, unions, customers, banks, or any dependent with which we exchange frequently. This material is based largely on the work of Fisher and Ury (1981).

We deliberately define a *successful* negotiation as one in which both parties are so satisfied with the agreement that this produces a minimum of problems with execution of the deal. Hence, a successful deal is one that is smoothly executed.

Broadly, a win-win strategy contains four steps:

1. intelligence gathering
2. preliminary discussions
3. negotiation planning
4. the negotiation itself

We will discuss each in turn.

Intelligence Gathering

■ The recently promoted materials manager of a medium-sized chemical manufacturer decided to negotiate a lower price for a certain raw material. A meeting was set up, and on the morning of the meeting, she called her stores manager and the production engineer in charge of the plant that used the raw material in question. She asked them to meet her at the offices of the supplying company. The three of them sat down to discuss the matter with two supplier representatives. As soon as the materials manager started discussing price, one of the supplier's representatives said that the price would be influenced by quality. To the material manager's horror, her production engineer started arguing for an increase in quality. Then, the other supplier's representative said that delivery costs were increasing, which could influence delivery performance. The materials manager started to feel the pressure when her stores manager started demanding that current delivery performance not only be maintained but also be improved. Somehow, she found toward the end of the negotiation that she had four people against her, instead of two. She eventually beat a hasty retreat after conceding a small price increase in exchange for a number of equally small improvements in quality and delivery. In discussing the matter some weeks later, she recognized that this disastrous event was her own fault for not considering the perspectives of the people she had asked along and for not discussing the issues with them beforehand.

Negotiate with Your Own Company First.   The point to be taken from this example is that when many individuals are involved in a negotiation, each one of them brings with him a unique perspective that influences his stand on, and attitudes toward, the issues raised. Therefore, it is vital to know ahead of time, particularly in the case of a team of negotiators, what stand is to be taken on the issue that will arise.

Intelligence gathering should begin at home, with the negotiator's own company. Issues, objectives, and priorities should be negotiated with any and all internal stakeholders. Walkaway positions and alternatives should be discussed and agreed to, as should who will be on the negotiating team and what their roles will be. Finally, the negotiator must have management's full commitment in three areas. First, for the period he is actually negotiating, he must be allowed to give the negotiation his full attention; he cannot afford to be distracted from an important negotiation by other issues. Second, he *must* be allowed a realistic deadline; and third, he and management must be clear on the limits of his authority. He cannot afford to renege on agreements he has made because his superiors overruled him. This destroys the trust needed to bind commitment to execution.

Do Your Homework. A good negotiator will also arm himself with as much information as possible regarding the target. This will include reviewing annual reports, 10Ks, press clippings, and any other sources that will enable him to analyze the *target's* needs, issues and attitude toward risk, and priorities. Further, one needs to know the character of the opposing team members: Are they impulsive or rational? Are they a single bloc, or do they have different members representing different interests? What alternatives do they have? What resources do they have? What tactics do they tend to employ? Does one person have the final say? Are they lackeys or principals?

Identify Other Interests. Identification of outside stakeholders should be made, as well as their stakes in the outcomes. We cannot afford to have a good deal blocked by our target's union or by our bank, for example. We must search for information on who (other than the primary parties) might have a stake in the outcome and whether they can interfere or help directly or indirectly in the negotiating process. A good negotiation makes good use of those who would help and disarms or neutralizes those who could hinder the bargaining.

Preliminary Discussions

Preliminary discussions should be held to decide who will attend, to select any experts, and to determine whether other parties should be notified and what the key issues will be. Here, much can be learned, or confirmed, of the target's needs, issues, and priorities as well as areas of common ground, problem areas, and possible stakeholder interests. Much of what is achieved in these preliminary discussions is confirmation of the assumptions made in the intelligence gathering stage.

Negotiation Planning

Once the preliminary discussions have yielded the information required by both sides, they should break off and give way to serious planning prior to and in anticipation of the formal bargaining sessions. Again, the first step is analysis.

In complex negotiations, many issues arise. The first step in any issue analysis is trying to determine ahead of time what the issues will be, so that negotiations do not become deadlocked over the unexpected appearance of an issue. In this regard, it is important to try to view the negotiation from the point of view of the targets, as well as of the team preparing for the negotiation.

Once the key issues have been identified, it is essential to rank these issues in the order of importance to the negotiating team. It is in this rank-ordering process that much of the conflicts of interest within the team are likely to arise, thus providing the first useful product of the rank-ordering process. Rank ordering is by no means a simple process; but the more complex the problem, the more worthwhile it is to give the matter specific attention.

For example, the first column in Table 3.2 lists the issues that arose in the negotiation of a supplier contracting for the supply and construction of a new chemical facility to a customer. In the second column we see that the issues have been ranked in order of importance to the supplier. After having first identified the issues that would arise and what their relative importance was, it was useful to look at the same issues and rank order them in terms of the *target's* priorities (the third column).

When we put the two sets of priorities together, we see some interesting differences. We see that some issues that are very important to the supplier (such as price, terms, and subcontractor control) are of much less importance to the customer, while other issues of great importance to the customer (such as guarantees and service) are of much less importance to the supplier. Finally, delivery is important to *both*, while commissioning and design changes are not very important to *either*.

Table 3.2   Estimated Priorities of Issues in Negotiation

Issue	Importance to Supplier	Importance to Customer
Price	1	4
Delivery	2	2
Terms of payment	3	5
Subcontractor management	4	8
Design changes	5	6
Service after sale	6	3
Performance guarantees	7	1
Commissioning	8	7

There are several important connotations to this asymmetrical set of priorities. First, the fact that something is important to the customer but not to the supplier (such as performance guarantees) can be used to lever concessions out of the customer on an issue that is important to the supplier (such as price or terms of payment). To give in to the target prematurely because it is not important to the negotiator, is to lose this valuable source of leverage.

Second, the order in which issues are negotiated becomes important. Often, the first few items on the agenda are relatively unimportant to both parties. This gives the negotiators a chance to test one another's attitudes and styles. The behavior of the targets at this stage can be an important indication of their attitude toward the negotiation in general.

Third, the order in which issues are negotiated can provide useful signals for the negotiators. Suppose that the suppliers want to use their leverage on performance guarantees to obtain a better price. Then, if they can arrange to have performance guarantees placed ahead of price in the agenda, they can put up some very strong resistance in discussions of performance guarantees. After this resistance has been going on for some time, they can suggest that "maybe we can reach agreement on guarantees after price has been discussed." The implications are that if the customer gives on price, they might be prepared to give on performance guarantees.

Fourth, no matter how integrative the negotiating situation, some issues are very important to both parties. It is here that the key bluffs, threats or promises (or a combination of these) that we discussed before will have to be focused. If we cannot find ways of developing commitments to our positions on these issues, we shall inexorably be dragged down to our negotiating base—the lowest deal we would accept.

It is usually inappropriate to discuss issues that are really important to both parties until other issues have been settled, and some investment of time and energy in the process has been made, so that there is a commitment to striking a deal.

The order of issue discussion (or agenda) is so important that many negotiations are preceded by a negotiation of the agenda itself.

■ In international negotiations, such as the Paris peace talks between the United States and North Vietnam, considerable time was devoted to negotiating how the negotiations were to take place. Similarly, in many labor-management negotiations, there are prenegotiation sessions during which the agendas are negotiated informally. Once the issues have been identified and the priorities have been assigned to them, the negotiating team is in position to decide what stands it will take on the various issues and what its bargaining base will be for each issue.

Two more important steps in the planning process are: Plan a major *theme* and introduce a *deadline*.

■ The theme, whether it involves cost, quality, or any other issue important to the target, can be used to negotiate trade-off ("You must understand that quality will suffer if the price drops below what I'm asking") and, by its repetition, to demonstrate the negotiator's own integrity and concern for the target's positions.

■ It is also important to try to achieve (apparent) *control of the deadline*. Try to ensure that the target's deadline runs out earlier than yours, because this can give you a significant edge in the process (Cohen 1980). If, for example, a supplier knows that a certain customer must have the supplier's parts by a certain date or miss delivery of a large order, the supplier is much less pressured than the customer.

Fisher and Ury (1981) go so far as to suggest that the well-prepared negotiator has carefully considered all alternatives to the bargained for event, has chosen the one best alternative to a negotiated agreement, and has examined and developed it to the point of smooth implementation should it be necessary. This accomplishes two things. One, he is more comfortable and less stressed going into the session and, as a result, is less likely to make unwise agreements. And two, the target, seeing the negotiator's strong commitment to the alternative, has a much clearer notion of what terms will be acceptable and which will merely drive the negotiator away from the table.

It is critical to identify and include in the formal bargaining all *implementation issues* that could arise. This contingency planning negotiates the key action steps for the execution stage, such as asking *who* will take *what* action if quality delivered is not to specifications, or who will notify whom and *when* delivery may be delayed. Careful identification of these issues in the planning stage *and their inclusion as issues in the bargaining stage* ensures that the agreement does not fall apart in the implementation stage.

Given a feeling for the issues and their priorities, and given the objectives that will specify the stand to be taken on each issue, we are finally in a position to discuss the negotiating plan.

The plan starts with a *specification of what is on and off the agenda* and the order in which the negotiating team would like issues to be discussed. If resistance to this order is expected, the most likely agenda is specified. With the team's accumulated knowledge about its target, it should try to identify which bluffs, threats, and promises will be necessary for it to make. At the same time, the team might try to identify the bluffs and threats that the target might try, so that they can prepare counterbluffs and disarm the threats.

As discussed earlier in complex negotiations, the negotiator should *develop a major theme* that will be the basis of the positions taken on key issues. For instance, in the example of a chemical plant contract discussed earlier, the supplier might develop a theme that focuses on their having the most reliable processing equipment in that particular business. Sticking to this theme (which meets two of the customer's highest priority issues: guarantees and after-sales service), the supplier can develop positions on higher prices, quicker payments, and control of subcontractors. The bluffs, threats, and promises required to support their demands on these issues will then all be cast in the light of their commitment to a highly reliable plant, good after-sales service, and somewhat flexible completion dates. Demands to reduce price can then be claimed to jeopardize quality of plant and service. Any demand to speed up delivery date can be argued to require additional charges. By sticking to a major theme of "quality at a good price," an overall thrust of the negotiation can be developed that gives the supplier's argument credibility, coherence, and consistency.

It is also important for the negotiator to position deadlines beyond that of the target. This can be done by declaring that "we are prepared to negotiate and willing to spend the time to do it right." It can be made clear to the target that the negotiator has considered the alternatives, wants a deal, and *hopes* it is with the target. (Thus, the implication is that there *are* alternatives but that the target is currrently the most desired alternative.) This also signals that the negotiator has time and inclination, shows commitment to a win-win outcome, *but keeps control of the deadline.*

A win-win tone is maintained by de-emphasizing the negatives and emphasizing the positive behavior.

Counterproductive behavior to be avoided:
1. Irritators ("That's not true." "I don't believe you.")
2. Attacking personalities (attack the issue, not the person)
3. Immediate counterproposals (which suggest you have not listened to or thought about the proposal at all)
4. Macho ultimata
5. Questions implying distrust ("Is that really the case?")

Productive behavior includes the following:
1. Behavior labeling (tell them what you are going to do, e.g., "I'm going to ask a question now.")
2. Motive commentary (and tell them *why* you are going to do it, e.g., "The reason I'm asking is . . .")
3. Stress agreements already reached (indirectly highlights the cost of not reaching agreement)

4. Summarize, review, check (make sure everyone has heard the same thing and still *remembers*)

5. Ask relevant questions (this puts people in a responding mode and elicits information)

6. Listen more than talk (*hear* the responses; be comfortable with silence)

It may also be important to have *credible breakout tactics* planned. Such tactics must be credible so as not to be seen as delaying or counterproductive, but they may have to be available for those moments when the negotiators feel the need for more time or information, or just to regroup.

Finally, as mentioned before, *implementation should be stressed.* This should specifically address what can go wrong; what actions will be taken, and when, if things do go wrong; how we will know when to take action; who will be contacted and who will assume authority and responsibility in each organization for taking the corrective action. If such contingency planning is not included in the negotiation, implementation problems will have to be *renegotiated* during execution. Remember, a *successful* negotiation is one that ensures implementation without difficulty. Since Murphy's law often applies, this requires solving the problems of execution *before* they occur.

Once the negotiation plan has been formulated, it is also important to specify the major checkpoints that will be used in the program of negotiation. If, at any stage in the negotiation, these checkpoints are not acheived (and this often happens), it is a signal for the negotiator to break off, if possible, and review progress to date with the purpose of reformulating the plan.

This approach to negotiating strategy reduces it from a complex, disrupted, and nonproductive confrontation between egos to a process of achieving mutually satisfactory agreements on outcomes that are smoothly executed.

SUMMARY: KEY CONCEPTS

1. When unilateral manipulation is not possible, negotiation becomes the strategist's tool.

2. Every negotiator enters a negotiation with a bargaining base and an aspiration base.

3. Negotiators will not concede as long as they feel that their targets may concede.

4. To avoid having to concede, it is necessary to formulate a commitment to the current offer. This is a bluff that the current offer is the last offer.

5. A bluff should have a loophole that can be used to break a deadlock.

6. A threat is a conditional bluff, and so a weak threat can be as viable as a strong threat, provided that the commitment to carry out the threat can be demonstrated.

7. A promise is a self-commitment that negotiators need to make in a situation in which they can cheat.

8. For a promise to be effective, some system of monitoring and punishing cheaters is necessary.

9. A successful negotiation is one in which both parties are sufficiently pleased with the agreement and which, therefore, produces smooth execution. This requires that issues of implementation also be negotiated.

10. Win-win negotiating strategies are appropriate to the maintenance of long-term business relationships.

11. Win-win strategy contains four steps: intelligence gathering, preliminary discussions, negotiation planning, and the negotiation itself.

12. In complex negotiations, issue analysis is necessary, particularly to determine the relative priorities of issues between targets.

13. In formulating a negotiation plan in the face of high complexity, a major theme should be developed and pursued throughout the negotiation. Tactics can be developed to support the theme.

4

Managing Internal Stakeholders

So far we have discussed the ways and means for the strategist to build power and influence, and to develop negotiating skills. These bases and skills are not without targets. The strategist will have to use them to manage key stakeholders (those who can make or break the plan) if the strategy is *ever* to be effectively implemented.

In this chapter, we present the concepts and applications necessary for the identification and management of *internal* stakeholders. In the next, we do the same for *external* stakeholders.

This chapter starts with a discussion of the nature of internal politics. It then moves to a study of individual political behavior, the formation of informal coalitions, and finally the implications for strategy formulation.

THE NATURE OF INTERNAL POLITICS

In this section, our deliberate political perspective focuses on the internal processes operating in organizations. An understanding of the political content of organizational behavior is essential to the formulation of *implementable* strategies. First we explain the major types of relationships that exist between the organization and its environment, because the maintenance and management of these relationships are key to the management of internal and external stakeholders. The arguments in this section are drawn primarily from the conceptual work of March and Simon (1957), Cyert and March (1963), and Thompson (1967).

In all but the most primitive circumstances, "players" in a society are highly dependent upon other players for their survival. Few individuals are self-sufficient enough to be able to provide all the input that they require for physical and emotional health. In the same way, no firm or other type of organization has complete command of all the resources necessary for its well-being.

All organizations are dependent upon the environment for the provision of certain inputs, which the organization then transforms into outputs, which, in turn, are used to get more inputs. Organizational environmental relations thus tend to show a general pattern of input/transformation/output.

However, the inputs that are provided are generally scarce. Raw materials, labor, funds, and customers are not unlimited, and there are many other organizations in the environment that compete for those inputs. The successful political strategist understands the dynamics of the input exchange and the competition for such inputs.

For instance, a software development firm must have programmers. If it provides a satisfactory work environment with adequate compensation, *as perceived by the programmers*, the programmer wants the job. Hence, to meet their wants, the programmer and the firm *must* cooperate in exchanging labor for payment. The conflict arises over the *amount* of the exchange. The firm might try other programmers, and the programmer other firms. However, if both are to have their needs satisfied, there must be some software development firms and some programmers. Dependents cannot do without one another. The nature and degree of the conflict change with the balance of numbers; the more such firms and the smaller the pool of programmers, the more bargaining power shifts to the programmers, and vice versa.

Inducement-Contribution Exchanges

The organization exchanges its output for inputs. To simplify the discussion, let the exchange be regarded as the giving of an inducement for a contribution. For instance, an employer may exchange a salary (inducement) for an employee's labor (contribution). Alternatively, a retailer may exchange a product (inducement) for a customer's money (contribution).

This inducement-contribution agreement between the two parties must be acceptable to *both*. The *organization* decides whether the *contribution* it is receiving is sufficient for the inducement it is offering, which is determined by the offers it can receive from alternative dependents.

On the other hand, it is the *exchange partner* who decides whether the *inducement* being offered is sufficient for the contribution it is required to make. This, too, is determined partly by the alternative inducement-contribution offer the exchange partner receives from the competitors of the organization.

Unless both the organization and the dependent believe that such an agreement will be beneficial and of fair value, relative to the alternatives available, agreement will not be reached. Quite naturally, under conditions of scarcity of resources, the exchange partners attempt to obtain as high an inducement as possible and simultaneously attempt to give as low a contribution as possible. In such exchanges, one of the strategies the organization can employ is to use its resources to restructure the situation in such a way that the exchange partners are induced, coerced, persuaded, or obligated to provide the required support. An above-average benefit package, for instance, might induce employees, that might otherwise go elsewhere, to remain with the company.

Alternatively, by using the resources at its disposal, the organization can block the access of the exchange partners to its competitors or block access of competitors to exchange partners. In a period of high unemployment, for example, one firm offered job contracts to highly qualified engineers, which not only served as an inducement at the time but also effectively protected it from loss of key employees later when the job situation eased and became a lot more competitive.

INDIVIDUAL POLITICAL BEHAVIOR

The political behavior of individuals in the organization strongly affects its ability to effect beneficial exchanges. To anticipate and plan for internal support or resistance to the proposed action, the strategist must first understand the nature of individual political behavior. Individuals join, and submit to the authority of, organizations because they hope to achieve more long-term benefits than they would by not joining. In essence, individuals in the organization carry out manipulation, bargaining, and coalition activity, not only in their own interests, but also sometimes in the interest of a coalition to which they belong, and of the organization as a whole.

In accordance with their personal hierarchy of needs, individuals allocate their scarce resources to the attainment of these needs. However, this allocation of resources need not be confined purely to the satisfaction of current needs but can also be attuned to the creation of conditions in the individuals' environment that will reduce the uncertainty of the future satisfaction of these needs.

If individuals perceive that the actions of others will influence the attainment of these needs, they can behave as small political systems in their own right by acting against those players who influence their potential need satisfaction via manipulation or accommodation. We are concerned here with the behavior of individuals who do not accept their lot but try to achieve their ends in the face of actions by others that would influence these ends, namely, the political behavior of an individual.

Individuals have values that set limits on what actions they *will* take, as well as a certain measure of political capability in their situation that sets limits on what actions they *can* take. The extent to which they can perceive opportunities and threats and the extent of their political capabilities determine the extent of their political action. People who do not or cannot perceive threats and opportunities may tend to operate in a far less political way than people who do. People with little political capability may not be able to exploit the opportunity or avert the threats that they perceive.

In joining organizations, individuals subject themselves to the authority of the organization (within limits) to exercise power and influence over them. The organization as a whole can make certain binding decisions regarding the expected behavior of individual members and how those individuals must act for the accomplishment of the organization's goals. However, individuals submit to organizational authority only to the extent that they feel that doing so improves their chances of attaining their own goals. While they remain members of the organization, individuals can act politically in three ways:

1. They can act as their own agent to increase their own political capability both in the overall organization and in their own interest groups.

2. They can act as the agent of their interest groups to increase the political capability of their own interest groups (provided this increase in political capability does not detract from their own, in which case they may resist).

3. They can act as an agent of the organization to increase the political capability of the organization as a whole, to ensure its survival and success, and to support any proposed action that will improve the organization's status (provided this increased political capability does not detract from their own or from that of their interest groups, in which case they may resist).

It can be seen that members of an organization can be subjected to loyalty conflicts regarding their own interests, those of the groups, and those of the organization.

INFORMAL COALITIONS

As we have seen in the preceding section, one of the options frequently available to political players is to align themselves with an internal interest group to join an informal coalition. We distinguish between *formal* (formally formed and sanctioned by the organization) and *informal* (formed by individuals outside of the organization's formal structure). As discussed later in the chapter, the formation of formal coalitions is one of the options open to strategists to counteract the effects of the informal coalition.

The Evolution of Informal Coalitions

Since individuals in an organization seldom have the necessary power and influence to dictate to their organization, if they wish the organization to carry out actions that they desire, their power and influence must somehow be enhanced. We have pointed out that one of the bases of power is control of alternatives. Coalitions form because by doing so, they reduce the alternatives available to the organization. In an extreme case, the firm has great power with respect to the individual worker and can play one worker off against another, but if all workers unite to form a coalition (a union, for example), the alternatives available to the organization are reduced back to one monolithic, and thus powerful, unit. In the same way, a chief executive may be able to coerce her senior managers individually, but if they form a coalition stating that they will all resign if the firm does not expand its facilities instead of diversifying, the chief executive's power against this collective demand of her managers is reduced considerably.

However, coalition formation has its own problems. Members do not join the coalition without bringing with them their own demands, and the support of these coalition members could easily be given to alternative coalitions if the demands are not met. In effect, then, a coalition creates a small-scale suborganization in the broader organization. Each coalition must defend itself from competition for its members from other coalitions. Consequently, members of the group will be able to make demands on the coalition in exchange for their support. These demands are related to the individual members' goals and form two broad classes: demands on the coalition to satisfy the *current* wants and needs of the individuals, and demands that are related to the individuals' desire to ensure the *future* satisfaction of their needs and wants.

This second set of demands is of special interest. Each member of the coalition would like to see the coalition set certain goals, which if achieved would promote the individual's goals.

- For instance, one individual, concerned with infringements on his personal time, demanded that the coalition set a goal of increasing staff, rather than increasing pay, before he would provide support. Increasing staff would cause a reduction in overtime, which fitted in with his personal goals.

- A group of newspaper reporters were trying to get one of the more influential reporters to join them in their attempts to get more pages in the newspaper issues. She would not provide this support unless they agreed to the demand that some of the extra pages be devoted to articles and reports of interest to working women, since she felt strongly that the paper was underrepresenting this area, which was of great personal interest to her.

Each member of a coalition will, therefore, make a set of demands on the coalition to commit itself to certain goals. To obtain or retain the support of its members, the coalition as a whole must try to satisfy these demands by making commitments to pursue these goals. However, it is often impossible for the coalition to satisfy the demands of all of its coalition members, since by nature, individuals are so varied that their goals can never be perfectly congruent. To overcome this problem, the coalition as a whole can develop a set of commitments that are phrased in general, rather than in specific, terms. Because they are not too specific, they ensure the support of more members (who see room for their own goal achievement). These commitments to strive for generalized goals are defined as policy commitments (discussed in depth in Chapter 5).

Consider the case of the group of reporters in the earlier example. While all of the reporters were seeking to have the size of the paper increased, there were several subgroups, each of which had its own ideas as to who would get the increase. If the commitments of the group leaders had been phrased in specific terms, stating that they would press for X pages of extra sports coverage and Y pages of political coverage, they would have lost the support of the woman reporter. Instead, they committed themselves to pressing for a general increase in the size of the paper, in which space for sports, politics, women's interests, and several other topics would be decided later. In this way, they retained the support of many more coalition members that they would have had if they had been more specific. The main point was to *get* the concession from management; then it would be possible for members to start jockeying for space for their particular interests.

Coalitions are formed in the first place because the organization does not have the resources to provide for the complete satisfaction of all the members' goals. Therefore, people join coalitions to try to persuade the organization to pursue directions that suit their goals. If everyone were in the coalition, they would be back where they started. In his analysis of political coalitions, Riker (1962) argues that coalitions strive to reach the smallest size required for the coalition to get their way, since each share of the "spoils" that have to be divided up between the winners is greater. If we consider the reporters' coalition discussed earlier, this argument applies. The more people the reporters get in their coalition, the fewer pages left per coalition member once these extra pages have been "extracted" from the management.

In summary, coalition members make demands on the coalition to strive for certain goals, and the coalition as a whole makes policy commitments to its members in response to these demands. The coalition members must then decide whether these policy commitments are acceptable enough to warrant supporting the coaltion.

Potential members of a political coalition will join that coalition and contribute their resources only if they feel that the policy commitments of the coalition will promote their own goals. They will be content to stay with the political coalition only as long as the coalition appears to be realizing these policies and is successful. If members' requirements are not met, they may seek membership in an alternative coalition. Members that the coalition gains must be protected from the enticements of competing coalitions.

Emergence of Fiduciary Roles and Political Leaders

In complex political situations, the issues are messy and lack concreteness. The implementation of the policy commitments regarding these issues can be an extremely lengthy process (for instance, the creation of law and order in a big city). Since not all issues can be resolved simultaneously, the coalition, having limited resources, must pay attention to the more urgent issues and postpone less urgent ones until resources are available. How does the coalition determine which issues are urgent? Urgency is, to some extent, determined by the intensity of the coalition members' demands for attention to the issue.

A large amount of interaction must take place between all coalition members before the issues can be decided. In complex situations, in which large numbers of people are involved, it is impossible for them all to bargain simultaneously with each other regarding the issues involved, yet somehow these issues *must* be resolved! A situation like this results in the evolution of a more sophisticated political structure. By a process of differentiation, certain players in the situation assume specific political roles, and a hierarchical structure develops.

What basically happens in large organizations is that members of coalitions tend to allocate to one of their members a *fiduciary* role— a role in which the authority to make decisions for the coalition as a whole is vested in one person, who then acts as a representative of the group's interests in communications with other groups. This person may or may not be a formal manager of the group members. If the subordinates feel that a manager is not representing their interests well enough, they may elect a fiduciary among themselves to represent them against the manager or even to represent them over the head of their manager.

Fiduciaries are political players who represent an underlying coalition. Their role is to use the power of influence placed at their disposal by the coalition to manipulate or to accommodate other coalitions' fiduciaries. In the process of representing their interest group, fiduciaries may form supercoalitions with other fiduciaries, pooling resources with them. Depending upon the relative power of the participating fiduciaries, the rewards reaped by these supercoalitions will be allocated to the respective underlying coalitions that make up the supercoalitions. However, since the securing of such rewards may involve a considerable time lag, the fiduciaries also demand policy commitments on the issues that are of interest to their underlying groups.

Since the interests of all coalitions are not identical, the fiduciaries choose to bargain only with those fiduciaries whose policy demands are not mutually exclusive to theirs. They will compete with the others.

In large organizations, supercoalitions bargain or compete with other supercoalitions, thus forming ever-larger coalitions in which fewer and fewer fiduciaries interact, each one representing the interests of larger and larger numbers of coalitions and their underlying beneficiaries. Eventually, the whole system of individuals will be characterized by a hierarchy of coalitions that culminates in a few major coalitions, some with directly opposing interests. When we recall the way in which organizations develop formal specialized subsystems (functions, divisions, departments) to deal with complexity, it is not surprising that these formal subsystems, with their narrower perspectives and rather specialized goals, often also form the major coalitions.

Thus, in any organization, we might find the "marketing people" and the "production people" who have their interests represented by a few powerful and influential representatives from the respective departments. Depending on the relative power and influence of these major departments, one or the other might be able to have its way on the issues that are being faced in the organization.

Problems with Coalitions

Instead of proceeding from an existing coalition, assume that there are numerous individuals who have not yet formed coalitions. It is virtually impossible for an individual to achieve all his goals using only his own resources; he is dependent upon the cooperation of other individuals to achieve many of them. If all the players in a situation had completely similar goals, coalition formation would present no problems; the coalition would consist of all the players. All that would have to be decided would be the final allocation of the rewards gained from the coalition's activities. This allocation would be accomplished by a multiperson bargaining process. However, in the more realistic case, in which the goals of actors are not congruent, competitive coalitions arise. Hence, despite the fact that a group of players may have a large number of common goals, the formation of a grand coalition of all the players is prevented by players who have perhaps a few conflicting goals and so make conflicting demands. Separate coalitions form when groups of individuals start taking sides on such issues.

The priority with which issues are considered may have a significant effect on the way in which coalitions are formed. Furthermore, it is not inconceivable that an uneasy alliance of enemies can join together with the express purpose of stopping a decision from taking place via a blocking coalition.

IMPLICATIONS FOR STRATEGY FORMULATION

For a number of reasons, the political strategist cannot afford to ignore the political action in organizations in the formulation of strategy. In this chapter, we have addressed the first of them: Political strategy is formulated in the context of the strategist's own organization; internal considerations place constraints on what strategies the formulator is *allowed* to use.

■ One of the major frustrations that President John F. Kennedy experienced in the Cuban missile crisis was discovering that at the time of the crisis, the Jupiter missiles in Turkey, which he had ordered to be removed some time before, were still in place. His direct order had not been executed for weeks because interest groups found ways of delaying implementation.

■ A major agricultural importer decided to implement a program whereby its producing lands would be turned over to nationals in the country of production. The decision to do this was announced at the head office as a formal policy decision, but it took years to implement because of the resistance by the local management at the regional level.

■ The soap manufacturer discussed in an earlier chapter was forced to postpone plans to diversify into food production because of the resistance of a powerful group of managers who demanded expansion of the soap production operation.

All of these examples are manifestations of situations in which internal political processes delayed or prevented the execution of a major policy decision. It is well to recognize the internal politics of an organization before selecting a course of action.

Organizations rarely reach a political position that permits them unilaterally to dictate action in their entire environment. There are so many exchange partners and competitors that the limits of the organization's political capability will be reached long before it has subjugated every exchange partner and every competitor. Therefore, it is particularly important to focus scarce resources in a manner that allows for their most effective use. To that end, a stakeholder impact analysis is required.

Stakeholder Impact Analysis

Any organization has a multitude of internal and external stakeholders. For purposes of discussion, we define stakeholder as an individual, a coalition of people, or an organization whose support is essential or whose opposition must be negated if a major strategic change is to be successfully implemented. Stakeholders can include a corporate parent company, stockholders, key personnel, individual competitors, the employee body, a strong supplier group, a strong buyer group, the government, and affected special interest groups, to name a few. While the ability to manage them all is a necessity in the long run, few organizations have the resources required to manage all stakeholders during each and every strategic change. It is critical in the strategy formulation process to identify those stakeholders who will be affected most by the strategy and to formulate political strategies for their management *or*, if they cannot be managed, to alter the strategy as required. To accomplish this, a stakeholder impact analysis is essential.

A form such as the one in Table 4.1 can prove helpful both in the determination of key stakeholders and in the formation of political strategies for their management. Its strength lies in obtaining answers to a series of questions:

1. Who are the stakeholders?
2. What are their interests and concerns?
3. As a result, what demands are they likely to make of the organization?
4. What are the resultant strategic challenges?
5. What action is necessary to neutralize the resistors, and to capitalize on the supporters? Is this action possible? (If not, revise strategy.)

Once the first four questions have been answered, key stakeholders can be identified by the strength of their possible impact, and the last question, with its implications for resource allocation decisions, can be addressed.

Throughout the strategy formulation process, the stakeholder impact analysis should be updated as new stakeholders emerge.

Building Commitment

The question that frequently arises is whether political processes should or can be eradicated in a formal organization. Political processes are spontaneous, natural, and necessary phenomena in the organization. It is via political processes that the demands from the

Table 4.1   Stakeholder Impact Analysis

Stakeholders	Interests and Concerns	Demands	Strategic Challenges	Action Plans

environment and from the organization's members are articulated. The chief executive cannot respond to all the demands being placed upon the organization. A well-managed political process provides a filter for all but the most important demands, provided that the chief executive understands the nature of political action. In essence, the chief executive (or any manager on a smaller scale) has a responsibility to control and channel political activity to the benefit of the organization. To attempt to stamp out politics is also to deny organizations the flexibility necessary to adapt to changing internal and external pressures.

The key to control of organizational politics lies in developing an ability to analyze organizational action in a political context. The strategist has to be aware of the major coalitions within the organization, and of the power and influence of both internal and external interest groups. A knowledge of where the power and influence lies, and where it will lie, enables the strategist to anticipate political action and take steps to control this.

In their studies of middle management coalitions, MacMillan and Guth (1985) conclude that the importance of gaining coalitions' commitment cannot be overemphasized. They suggest that the implications for general management in the strategy formulation process are fourfold:

1. Recognize the political realities and manage them
2. Learn to use the classic political tools
3. Manage coalition behavior
4. Take action against opposing coalitions

The first point has already been covered in this chapter. The last three bear further explanation.

Use Classic Political Tools.   A number of political management tools, used by politicians for centuries, are available to general managers for use in gaining commitment and, hence, formulating and implementing strategy in their organizations.

Equifinality.   Recognize that the end is more important than the means. Good strategists should recognize that an alternate path that offers higher levels of internal commitment, and which would not be blocked by internal stakeholders, may be preferable to the one they propose.

Satisficing, or seeking a solution that is satisfactory to all, is better than the "best" one in the eyes of the strategist.   While there is a fine line between satisficing and suboptimal compromise, the strategist facing low commitment and resulting low implementation rate may prefer *some* results to *no* results.

Generalization. Generalization involves a movement away from the specific, back to the general issue, for example by seeking "enhanced productivity" rather than "cost cutting by reducing overtime." When the means of achieving the goal can be entrusted to the internal stakeholders rather than directed by the strategist, the increase in commitment attained can often allow the organization to reach a goal that might otherwise have been unattainable.

Focus on higher-order issues. By showing stakeholders how the failure of the strategy might seriously affect the firm in the long run, the strategist can often raise the level of commitment.

Anticipate and Manage Coalition Behavior. Recognizing that coalitions form around issues, astute strategists can study recent and current coaltions, their membership, their issues, and their success rate. Such an analysis allows strategists to anticipate what coalitions will form and what may be their membership, and consequently to plan ahead for their management. Several methods of doing so are discussed next.

Manage the sequence in which issues are addressed. To a large extent, coalitions tend to form around issues. By controlling which issues will be given emphasis and which priorities will be attached to these issues, strategists can channel political activity in directions they feel better suit the organization's interests. Think back on any of the recent presidential campaigns, and consider the extent to which the candidates attempted to raises issues before the nation and to attract public attention to issues that suited them rather than their targets. Consider how public opinion shifted as each candidate pushed favorable issues for himself into the public eye and forced the less successful target to defend himself against these issues.

Increase the visibility of certain issues. In a careful selection and avoidance of issues addressed in formal and informal communications, the strategist can focus total organization attention on areas in which the coalition is vulnerable and thus neutralize its effects.

Unbundle issues into smaller subissues. The less important the subissue, the more unimportant the time and energy required to form and manage the coalition becomes. To the extent that strategists can successfully reach their goals by slow and small implementation steps, the more success they will enjoy in implementing the entirety.

Take Direct Action Against the Opposing Coalition. Stronger measures may be called for at certain times.

Form preemptive or countercoalitions. Political strategists, in a move to preempt or counter the anticipated coalition, may create a coalition of their own in an attempt to neutralize the impact. This relies on gaining commitment from the stakeholder group by including some of its key members in either the formulation or the implementation process.

Change the organizational position of opposing coalition leaders. Repositioning can, in effect, behead the coalition, since the power or influence base available to the coalition leaders is to a great extent a function of their position within the organization.

Co-opt coalition members. Similar to the formation of formal coalitions, coopting members relies on educating or "buying out" a key member or anticipated member of the opposing coalition.

Increase persuasion efforts with coalition members. To the extent that the coalition's issues are a result of lack of understanding, an increase in the communication effort may be sufficient to disperse the group.

Remove coalition leaders from the organization. Once a stand has been taken, coalition leaders, in particular, have strong emotional and political reasons for continued resistance. Their removal may be the only option.

The Difference Between "Winning" and the "Right Way"

Strategists are often guilty of the same self-interested behavior they find so frustrating in internal coalitions. They, after all, have invested a great deal of time and energy in the formulation process and, as a result, may have a personal stake in the issues. As a final caveat in this chapter, we suggest that the political strategist look closely at the relative importance of any disagreement. It is the degree of the importance of the decision that should determine the amount of the investment spent on restructuring the situation.

Rappaport (1960) argues that there are essentially three strategies for dealing with disagreement. *Conditioning*, generally available only to those holding power, utilizes negative sanctions whenever the target disagrees. Such a strategy may result in eventual behavior change but will most certainly not result in a high commitment. The target is simply beaten. This utilizes the negative manipulation mode covered in Chapter 2.

A second strategy involves explaining to targets their "false image" of reality. This may be successful where there is no fundamental disagreement and the target is willing to listen. Although utilizing the positive mode, this still involves "beating" the target.

The third strategy suggested by Rappaport may be called for when the issue is seen as vital to both parties. In essence, it is a strategy of debate in which each person explains their *targets'* points of view to the satisfaction of the targets. This method recognizes that there will be cases in which finding the *right way* is critical, thus making a major investment in finding it worth the expenditure. In that light, the win-win negotiating strategy discussed in Chapter 3 again emerges as an important tool in the strategy formulation process and gaining commitment from internal stakeholders.

A study by MacMillan and Guth (1985) showed that low commitment can stem from two major sources: Either the predicated outcomes of the strategy have low desirability or stakeholders have low confidence that the strategy will have the outcome predicted (or both of these). All possible combinations are illustrated in the matrix presented in Table 4.2.

Cell 1 presents no problem to strategists. Cells 3 and 4 suggest tactics presented in the prior section. The conditions in cell 2, however, should cause strategists to dissociate themselves from their personal stake in the issue, to stand back and look for *what* is right, rather than for *who* is right.

To summarize, then, strategists should make every attempt to approach areas of disagreement with an evaluation of the need for the right answer rather than the need to win, keeping a jaundiced eye on their own emotional investment in the process. Successful use of the third of Rappaport's strategies will, over time, gain strategists the respect of their targets and lower future resistance barriers.

Table 4.2

Level of Disagreement on Desirability of Outcomes	Level of Agreement on Methods to Be Used	
	Low	*High*
Low	High commitment 1	Low commitment to procedures 2
High	Low commitment to results 3	Low commitment to procedures and results 4

SUMMARY: KEY CONCEPTS

1. The organization's strategy will inevitably have some impact on its members. The political strategist must consider the nature of the demands that will be made by these internal stakeholders and, where appropriate, use its resources to restructure the situation in such a way that the stakeholders will provide the support necessary for implementation.

2. Stakeholder management is facilitated by an understanding of individual political behavior and an understanding of the process by which coalitions form and evolve.

3. Individuals and groups can behave as political actors in an organization by striving to restructure conditions such that the organization pursues goals that suit these individuals and groups.

4. These "players" tend to use manipulation, bargaining, and coalition formation with interest groups to achieve their purposes.

5. Coalitions tend to build around issues.

6. Some control of coalition structure may be achieved by making different issues visible.

7. To gain commitment from internal stakeholders, the political strategist must anticipate and manage coalition behavior.

8. The degree of importance of the proposed strategy should determine the amount of the investment spent on restructuring the situation and the direction of the restructuring effort. Gaining commitment should take the form of finding the "right way" rather than "winning," when the issues at hand are critical to the organization's success.

5

Managing External Stakeholders

Organizations do not exist in a void. Any number of external individuals and organizations have a stake in them, and these stakeholders will make self-interested demands on the organization. The power and influence of the stakeholders determine the need for political action on the part of the organization's management.

This chapter explores the nature of interorganizational political relationships, options for political action, and the implications for strategy formulation. This political strategy is concerned with reinforcing the economic strategy of the organization, for without a sound and viable economic strategy, the organization will not be able to retain environmental support over time. However, having decided on an economic strategy, the organization has to select from a number of political options in deciding how to execute this strategy.

THE NATURE OF EXTERNAL RELATIONSHIPS

Basically, external stakeholders fall into three categories in their relationship with the firm. They are either providers of input, or they are competing for the firm's providers of input, or they have some special interest in how the firm operates.

In the first category, we find not only suppliers but also buyers, financial institutions, the labor pool, and so on. The relationship that exists between the organization and these stakeholders is a symbiotic one that strongly influences their behavior in respect to one another, since the organization depends for its very survival upon these "dependents." The dependents in turn depend upon the organization to take their outputs; without the organization *or others like it*, the dependents could not survive. Consequently, the relationship between the dependents and the organization is one in which all must cooperate, even though they may be in conflict as to how to cooperate. This theme of conflict over cooperation captures the essence of the way in which dependents behave with respect to one another.

   ■ For instance, a manufacturing firm must have customers. If it is providing a desirable product, the customers want the product. To meet their wants, customer and firm must cooperate in exchanging product for payment. The conflict that arises is over the price of the exchange. The firm might try other customers and the customers might try other firms, but if both are to have their needs satisfied, there must be some manufacturers and some customers. Dependents cannot, or do not want to, do without one another.

In the second category, we find *competitors*, those actors in the environment that seek to attract the organization's dependents. These competitors may be *direct* competitors for customers, but they may also be other industries, banks, or even the government competing for other inputs (such as computer programmers, funds, or strategic raw materials). Competitors do not need one another to survive. While cooperation is possible, competitiveness better defines the nature of the relationship.

In the third category, we find *special interest groups:* any organization from the local PTA to the government, which is concerned with those aspects of the firm's operations that affect their interests. Due to the nature of the special interest, conflict most often defines the nature of this relationship; compromise rather than collaboration is more often the solution to the conflict. For ease of discussion, special interest groups will be considered part of the dependent category in the material that follows. The reader is encouraged to remember, however, when formulating strategies for their management, that actions appropriate for all dependents are not necessarily appropriate for all interest groups.

POLITICAL OPTIONS

In dealing with any of the three categories of external stakeholders, the firm must seek to create a control position for itself in the environment. Our discussion of the political options available to the firm in seeking control over its environment is based on the approach of Schumpeter (1942), Marchal (1951), Pfeffer and Salancik (1978), and Bacharach and Lawler (1980).

In Chapter 2 we said that the political capability of the firm depended on its political resources, that is, its power and influence bases. To secure future political capability, the firm can therefore attempt to expand or consolidate these bases.

Ideally, a firm should seek to structure conditions in the environment in such a way that the dependent with which it is exchanging has no alternative exchange partner in the situation, since such a condition ensures that the terms of exchange are best for the firm. Firms should strive to create such conditions in their environment, or at least near approximations to these conditions, to gain maximum power or influence in the situation. However, such gains are generally temporary, since elements in the environment can undertake political action to develop countervailing power to resist this control.

Political action of the firm seeks to create and exploit a series of temporary conditions in which it controls the environment and, as these controls are eroded by the reaction of the environment, to continuously create new control conditions.

There are a confusingly large number of ways in which the firm can undertake political action to create the control conditions it desires. To reduce the confusion, it is useful to classify these ways along four dichotomous "dimensions" of options. These dimensions are like branches in a decision tree and include the following decision points.

Target of Action

With the limited resources available to it, the firm must first decide on the target of its action: dependent or competitor. For example, a manufacturer might attempt to secure a long-term contract with a supplier (dependent), thus securing supplies and blocking off a competitor from their supplies. Or a group of companies (competitors) in an industry might form an employers' association for negotiating with unions, thus preventing the unions from playing one organization off against the others.

Whether to Act Directly or Indirectly

Having opted for action against a particular stakeholder, the strategist must now decide whether to take direct or indirect action. For example, a company may attempt to develop specific (direct) influence with key customers by co-opting members onto the board. Or it can purchase a critical raw material supplier and use this to control the behavior of its competitors (indirect).

Whether to Take Manipulative or Accommodative Action

It should be clear that both actions can be done. One may try to manipulate the situation to create the best conditions for accommodation. The "dimensions" are not mutually exclusive. A well-conceived political strategy can use combinations of political actions, such as simultaneously taking direct, accommodative action against dependents and indirect, manipulative action against competitors. But here we are primarily concerned with the broad types of options available. One of the broad options, then, is whether to act primarily by manipulation or by accommodation. Thompson (1967) conceived of several ways of accommodating with an element of the environment.

By Joint Commitment. By jointly committing themselves to a course of action, the firm and its target dependents or competitors come to agreement as to how they are going to behave in the future. A company can enter into a contract with one or more of its customers. For the length of that contract, the firm is assured of output and customers are assured of input. Alternatively, a company can enter into a joint agreement with its competitors regarding how they are going to handle unions or government agencies.

By Co-optation. By co-opting a powerful or influential member of the target organization into its policy-making processes, the firm confers on the target a certain amount of authority, but at the same time hopes that the target member will also consider the interests of the firm when she is participating in the policy formulation processes of the target organization. For instance, it is not uncommon to find the board of directors co-opting members who represent major creditors, such as banks.

By Coalescence. By coalescing, the organization and its target formally combine and pool their political resources against the environment. They both submit to the authority of the joint organization thus formed. For example, a merger between two competitors or a merger between a firm and a major supplier or customer combines the two organizations' financial, physical, and human resources and equips them both with more political capability in their environment than if they continued to act as separate organizations. However, the coalescence need not be permanent. In situations in which the individual organizations do not have the resources to meet a particular challenge in the environment, it is not uncommon for one or more competitors to form a consortium. Their resources are pooled until the challenge has been met, and then the consortium

Table 5.1 Representation of General Options Available to the Political Strategist

Target	Type of Action	Means of Action	Political Relations
Dependents	Direct	Accommodation	Existing
		Manipulation	Existing
	Indirect	Accommodation	Existing
			New
		Manipulation	Existing
			New
Competitors	Direct	Accommodation	Existing
		Manipulation	Existing
	Indirect	Accommodation	Existing
			New
		Manipulation	Existing
			New

disbands. Temporary organizations of this nature occur frequently in the case of large projects, such as construction or military projects, where several smaller companies combine to compete against the larger ones.

These three ways of mutual accommodation—joint commitment, co-optation, and coalescence—can be brought about by various means. In earlier chapters, we considered manipulation and negotiation. The techniques discussed there will be helpful here in formulating accommodative or manipulative action plans.

Whether to Act within the Existing Political Structure or to Expand It

Until now, the discussion has implicitly assumed that the firm has accepted the status quo and has confined itself to acting in the existing system. However, the firm may well attempt to create a new system.

By creating new political relations, the firm may be able to effect direct or indirect manipulation of dependents or competitors. For example, many firms facing situations of increasing government regulation have the choice of remaining in the industry (where they are almost powerless against the increasing demands of government agencies, however damaging to profits these demands may be) or of trying to find new areas of activity where the power balance is not so decidedly to their disadvantage. Many companies that traditionally supplied such industries are diversifying into other less controlled industries.

If we take four dimensions of possible action (and remove those that are mutually exclusive), it is possible to identify twelve major options available to the firm contemplating political action. These are depicted in Table 5.1.

NUMBER OF STAKEHOLDERS

The political action that the firm can undertake in its environment depends largely on the relative number of stakeholders in the environment. A simple representation of these conditions is given in Table 5.2.

By *few* we mean more than one dependent or at least one competitor. Many, on the other hand, is some arbitrary amount larger than, say ten, after which coordination and control of joint action become difficult.

Each situation in Table 5.2 gives rise to distinctive limits to the types of political action the firm can use.

It is possible (MacMillan 1972) to discuss in great detail the ways in which the structure of dependents and competitors limits the options and suboptions of political action available to the firm under each of the four conditions depicted in Table 5.2. This would be tedious, and the purposes of this book will not be served by such a detailed and long-winded analysis.

Instead, the major options available to a firm under various environmental conditions have been indicated in Table 5.3. Many of the options listed draw on economic and marketing concepts as well

Table 5.2   Major Conditions Under Which the Firm Must Take Political Action in Its Environment

Dependents	Competitors	
	Few	*Many*
Few	Bilateral oligopoly	Oligopsony
Many	Oligopoly	Perfect competition

Table 5.3 Key Options for Political Strategy Under Major Environmental Conditions

Target: Competitors	Many Competitors Many Dependents (Perfect Competition)	Few Competitors Many Dependents (Oligopoly)	Many Competitors Few Dependents (Oligopsony)	Few Competitors Few Dependents (Bilateral Oligopoly)
Direct Accommodation	Joint commitment via industry association; coalescence via merger of competitors	Joint commitment via pseudolegal agreements; coalescence of smaller competitors by merger or consortia	Joint commitment via industry associations; coalescence via acquisition of less efficient competitors	Joint commitment via industry association and pseudolegal agreements; coalescence of smaller competitors by mergers or consortia
Direct Manipulation		Inducement via side payments; coercion via threats; controlled erosion of competitors' power position		Inducements via side payments; coercion via threats; controlled erosion of competitors' power base
Indirect Accommodation		Develop signaling systems to stabilize industry		Develop signaling systems to stabilize industry
Indirect Manipulation		Seek indirect power and influence; seek new domains to reduce threat base of competitors		Actively seek indirect power and influences; seek new domains to reduce threat base of competitors
Target: Dependents				
Direct Accommodation	Joint commitment via contracting	Joint commitment via contracting	Joint commitment via contracting; co-optation of dependents	Joint commitment via contracting; vertical integration; co-optation of dependents
Direct Manipulation	Inducement via specialization in a narrow segment; persuasion and obligation via influence with target segment	Inducement via continuous differentiation of offering; coercion of controlled dependents; persuasion via mass communication; investments in publicity, philanthropy, intelligence systems	Inducement via specialization with specific dependents; persuasion via personal contacts; obligation via co-opted dependents	Inducement via specialization development; persuasion via personal contact; obligation via commitment of customers to product; investment in intelligence systems
Indirect Accommodation				Develop signaling systems to stabilize industry
Indirect Manipulation	Persuasion and obligation via influence over indirect dependents		Appeals to regulatory bodies; development of new domains to reduce dependents' dependence	Seek new domains to reduce threat base of dependents

as political concepts. The purpose here is to present a general array of possible options. Table 5.3 has proven useful for identifying the broad options available for developing a political strategy under each of the four different environmental conditions.

Reading down Table 5.3 indicates where the main thrust of political action could be made in each type of environment. For instance, a firm operating in an environment with many dependents and few competitors (column 2) could develop a political strategy that has one or more of the following components. (*These options should be considered only if legal in the country of reference.*)

1. Attempt to create a legal or pseudolegal system for obtaining joint commitments of competitors to issues that tend to disrupt the industry.

2. Be alert to opportunities to merge with competitors or form consortia.

3. Be prepared to reduce disruptive conflict between competitors by developing a suitable system of side payments for adhering to stabilizing agreements.

4. Develop a basis on which to threaten uncooperative competitors.

5. Formulate a strategy whereby the power base of the competitors is eroded rather than directly attacked, using the threat base and side payments to prevent retaliating action.

6. Develop a system of implicit signals that will be used to signal orderly changes in variables that could lead to disruptive action (for example, price leadership patterns, once recognized, prevent calamitous price wars).

7. Devote effort to analyzing and identifying major dependencies between competitors and their dependents so that their strengths and weaknesses are exposed.

8. Attempt to reduce the company's vulnerability to threat from competitors by developing new relations that either enhance the power and influence of the firm in the current situation or reduce the dependence of the firm on the current situation.

9. Use the power position of the company to secure favorable contracts from dependents.

10. Seek differentiation of the firm's offering from that of competitors.

11. Develop a subgroup of controlled dependents.

12. Seek audience via mass communication, publicity, and philanthropy.

13. Develop intelligence systems that will track shifts in dependents' perceptions and values, as well as competitors' actions.

This general strategy is substantially different from the one that could be adopted by conditions of columns 1, 3, or 4.

Several caveats are to be noted with respect to Table 5.3:

1. The list of options is by no means exhaustive.

2. The table represents a substantial oversimplification of environmental structure. The dichotomy of "few" and "many" leaves a lot of room for interpretation. However, the intention is to indicate where the main emphasis in political strategy formulation could be made.

3. *In all cases, do not assume that illegal action is being suggested.* Each option indicated should be treated strictly in terms of the specific legal constraints imposed by the society in which the reader operates.

4. Table 5.3 represents a single dependent/firm/competitor relation. Since there are many such relationships, it is possible that some of the actions suggested in the table could not be undertaken, in which case they would be excluded from the strategy.

5. The table provides only the general options for a political strategy. Whether a specific option is viable is a function of the expected response of elements in the environment. These expected responses can be developed by applying the concepts of stakeholder response as discussed next.

STAKEHOLDER RESPONSE

The viability of any strategic move should be judged not only from an economic perspective but also from the perspective of likely stakeholder response. The strength, weakness, and repercussions of that response are factors we must use to weigh the wisdom of each move.

Table 5.4 presents a summary of questions useful for anticipation and analysis of stakeholder response to strategic moves. Much of this material is based on MacMillan, McCaffery, and Van Wijk (1985) and Porter (1980). Each question in Table 5.4 is discussed in detail following the table.

1. What Are the Stakeholder's Goals and Focus?

What goals are they seeking, and which goals are being pursued with emphasis? Where is the current focus? How are these goals traded off against one another?

Table 5.4 Summary of Questions for Analyzing Possible External Stakeholder Responses to Strategic Moves

1. What are the stakeholder's current goals and focus? What have they been in the past?

2. Where are their major long- and short-term resources and policy commitments directed?

3. Are they satisfied with their current position, or is change likely? What changes are likely?

4. Where are they weak? Strong? In your eyes? In theirs?

5. What moves will provoke the greatest retaliation?

6. Are they inhibited from responding to strategic moves because:

   — to match the move would be counterstrategic?

   — the move is regarded as nonthreatening?

   — they are distracted by major problems or opportunities?

   — the move is not visible to them?

   — the threatened division has low priority in the larger organization?

   — no specific division is responsible or motivated to respond?

   — a correct response calls for major policy revision or costly revisions of procedures?

   — a response would create jurisdictional disputes and bureaucratic disruptions?

7. What are the stakeholder's own political issues?

■ If the organization we are moving against appears to be aggressively seeking market share and de-emphasizing profits, then a move on our part that threatens to have an immediate and highly visible impact on market share may elicit an immediate and aggressive response. Ways of making the move that are less obvious and have less immediate impact are likely not to be countered as aggressively. A firm in the travel industry announced its intentions of entering a new country with tours comparable to ones in which an established company dominated. This announcement was, within days, met by major reductions in prices and an increase in quality of existing tours by the dominant company, which was prepared to prune its profits considerably just to maintain its dominant position. However, if the aggressor had investigated further, it would have found that the dominant firm was concentrating its efforts only in the northern areas of the country. The new firm could have focused its initial efforts in the South, where the dominant firm's current business was obtained without direct marketing. The response of the dominant firm would have been much more restrained if the aggressor had focused initially in the South.

What Have the Stakeholder's Goals and Focus Been in the Past?

An understanding of the stakeholder's past can be helpful in understanding their present.

■ An organization known for its "slow follow" strategy in product introduction twice tried to enter the expensive game of product innovation. Both introductions were failures, and as a result, the firm's management will think long and hard before attempting to become the innovator again.

2. Where Are the Major Long- and Short-Term Resources and Policy Commitments Directed?

What are the major policy commitments that the target has made as to products, markets, distribution channels, promotion methods, and pricing? Where are the major shares of discretionary income being directed? To research, development, marketing, equipment? How are key personnel rewarded? What type of people are promoted? The point here is that the organization develops a momentum on the basis of the strategy it formulates, and this highly coordinated and massive movement of resource flows is difficult to redirect without a great deal of disruption. We saw in Chapter 2 that the commitment structure of the targets plays a major role in determining their influence base. The more one knows of their commitments to their own internal and external stakeholders, the more one can identify avenues of action from which they are precluded out of their obligation to keep their commitments to these groups. In the face of a strategic move that would make this redirection necessary, the target may decide to forgo the opportunity to counter this strategy.

■ An electronics equipment manufacturer developed a strategy in which it dominated the market through the development of high-quality, extremely reliable sophisticated equipment based on new technology. Initial users required these product characteristics, but only until they themselves came to grips with the new technology. Over time, user competence rose to the level that they could handle many of the problems of lower-quality, less expensive equipment themselves. However, the manufacturer was unwilling to abandon its "quality strategy," because the entire organization was geared to quality production. Its investments in equipment, its technicians and managers, and its contracts with suppliers all supported a quality product, and for this to be changed, massive efforts in developing new processes, buying new machinery, and redeveloping employees would have been necessary. Therefore, the response to the advent of lower-quality price competitors was to allow them to slowly erode market share.

What major investments is the target making? What is the structure of its immobile assets? Who is being trained, and what type of training is taking place? What major long-term contracts must it meet? What type of technology is it pursuing? Long-range commitments take a long time to bear fruition, and a great deal of funds and resources are tied up for considerable periods of time before profits start being generated. To terminate such commitments and redeploy the resources takes a great deal of courage, for not only does this often mean a total loss of all that has gone before, but also the process of readjustment can be extremely painful. The less accustomed to such decisions the target is, the more likely it is that it will persist in the course that has been set some years before in the hope that "things will turn out all right in the end."

■ Consider the case in which a building contractor waited until its major competitor was overcommitted on contracts before moving into the segment dominated by that competitor. At that point, all attention in the target organization was focused on coping with the large overload of contracts. When the aggressor did move, it focused its emphasis primarily on its ability to deliver contracts on time—at a stage when the target was powerless to respond in kind because it was overloaded and late on deliveries already.

■ Another equipment manufacturer invested most of its resources in staying ahead of competition in a certain electronics technology. Its major competitor, which was much smaller, made a breakthrough in a less advanced technology and has, since that time, been systematically consolidating its position and increasing its share of the market while it catches up on the advanced technology. To this day, the manufacturer has persisted in pursuing the advanced technology at enormous cost in the hope that once the breakthrough comes, it will reestablish dominance. Every month, the decision to abandon the advanced technology becomes more painful and difficult to make.

3. Are They Satisfied with Their Current Position, or Is Change Likely?

While financial performance is an obvious place to look for level of satisfaction, other indicators are available that will help anticipate the stakeholder's potential shift in focus. An analysis of the industry chain as outlined in Chapter 2 may also indicate impending change in the stakeholder's focus.

4. Where Are They Weak? Strong? In Your Eyes? In Theirs?

All organizations hold certain assumptions about themselves that may cause them to turn a blind eye to weaknesses and strengths that may appear obvious to others. If, for example, an organization prides itself on product quality, efforts aimed at besting them in the quality arena may provoke the greatest response. On the other hand, if they steadfastly refuse to recognize that their service or delivery is poor, it may be possible to make major inroads among disgruntled customers before the organization acknowledges their weakness.

5. What Moves Will Provoke the Greatest Retaliation?

The business press is rife with reports of severe competitive counter-moves precipitated by organizations that, knowingly or unknowingly, have threatened a competitor's prized domain. Organizations should think twice before attempting such a move. An area held dear by a competitor, for whatever reason, may be "held to the last person." The resulting wars of attrition can be enormously costly to both sides.

6. How Are They Inhibited from Responding?

The first three items listed under this question in Table 5.4 are self-explanatory. The remainder are usually caused by internal structure conditions. Organizations subdivide into specialist parts that handle specific subtasks (Lawrence and Lorsch 1967). By the very fact that they do subdivide, they create problems of ensuring that the many separate subtasks are coordinated and controlled.

1. The organization must *coordinate* the disparate demands for resources and ensure that the transfer of these resources from one department to another or from one subdepartment to another actually takes place; otherwise, instead of absorbing uncertainty, these departments create uncertainties for one another. This coordination problem of the organization results in the development of a large number of bureaucratic rules, procedures, policies, and programs, whereby the departments are instructed how to act under an array of specific conditions.

2. The organization must also *control* the activities of its departments to ensure that they (a) do not single-mindedly pursue their own subtasks to the detriment of the organization as a whole and (b) carry out these subtasks. To cope with this problem, the organization develops complex control systems that monitor the performance of the divisions, assess the performance, and then reward or punish the division according to how well the task has been performed.

The possible response of a target is influenced by these bureaucratic processes in many ways. A brief discussion of six such possibilities follows. The reader is referred to Chapter 6, Policy Formation as a Political Process, for more detail on this topic.

First, if the strategic move the organization makes is something that the target has never encountered before (as is often the case), the organization does not have a set of rules, policies, or procedures to cater to this move. In many cases, it may respond to the move by continuing as it has always done, or perhaps by countering the move in the nearest way it can find that "fits the rules." In particular, policies that emerge as the guidelines for behavior in response to demands from powerful internal and external stakeholders are difficult to change, and there is a tendency for organizations to persist in these policies.

■ For instance, a company may have committed itself to a policy of maintaining a specific liquidity level as a result of demands from its creditors. It can find itself in a difficult position if the move we make means that it must redeploy cash and thus reduce liquidity. This may be the time to launch a major sales promotion campaign, offering distributors major discounts for large orders.

Second, procedures and rules by which the organization monitors or "sees" its environment may be such that the organization fails to notice the move a competitor has made. An apparel company's move into the youth market went unnoticed by a major competitor because the competitor did not have a category in its sales analysis called "youth market."

Third, the time that it takes for information about the move to reach the decision-making level where a counterresponse can be generated can cause critical delays.

■ For example, a small low-cost producer used to "blitzkrieg" different areas of the household chemical market at different times. By the time the competitor's head office received information concerning the producer's inroads, it was too late to respond because he had already moved out of that region and into the next one.

Fourth, the way in which the organization assesses performance may influence whether the signal gets to the decision-making level that generates the response at all and in what form it gets there. Thompson (1967) argues that organizations (or their parts) will provide information on which they are assessed in forms that suit them. If an organization is losing market share in a growth market, it will prefer to be assessed on historical sales growth rather than on market share. Given the choice, the company may therefore choose to report historical growth rather than growth compared with its competitors.

Fifth, in designing the coordination of resources between divisions, the organization must make commitments of resources. It is, therefore, disruptive if a particular division unexpectedly makes additional demands for these resources. The demands disrupt the pattern that has been planned; sorting this out can create critical delays.

Sixth, the specific perspective of one department (say sales) may make the department rather unsympathetic to problems encountered in another department (say production). This lack of perspective on both parts often gives rise to parochial conflicts and conflicts of jurisdiction and authority as each department tries to "solve" the problem posed by the strategic move in terms of its frame of reference.

Therefore, in formulating some sense of the type of responses we can expect from our targets, it is important that we consider the following:

1. What types of major rules, procedures, policies, and programs are used by targets? These may influence the visibility of our move and the time it takes to recognize the move, and limit the responses they can generate.

2. What major monitoring and control systems does the target employ? How are departments evaluated? How often are they measured? How are people rewarded and punished? At what level in the organization are decisions relevant to our move made?

3. How is the target organized? What major departments does it have? Will the strategic move directly affect more than one department? Will it affect them in different ways? Are there likely to be conflicts between departments? How ingrained are the systems in these departments? What constraints are imposed on their actions by the organization?

The better the knowledge we have of these factors, the better we can assess the impact of strategic moves that we contemplate and the likely responses to them, given the time lags and coordination problems that would be experienced by the target as a result of the move.

7. What Are the Stakeholder's Own Political Issues?

What is the political structure of the stakeholder organization? What are the dominant coalitions? What is their source of power and influence? Are there any major countercoalitions? The results of this type of analysis will indicate the vulnerability of the organization to specific political moves. A political move could initiate a great deal of political turmoil within the organization if it is used as a "test of strength" by a major coalition. The analysis will also provide a sense of which alternative responses would be an anathema to the major stakeholders and which would be more acceptable.

What major demands are being placed on the organization? Which major external interest groups are making these demands? To which commitments are they currently paying attention? The analysis should provide a sense of what constraints are imposed on the organization and also what responses will be proscribed unless the organization can convince the relevant external groups to relax the constraints.

What is the discretion structure in the organization? Who can exercise discretion and at what level? How does the organization "treat" unsuccessful use of discretion? A knowledge of these factors provides a sense of the riskiness of various responses available to the target and the likelihood that some responses will not be considered because the proposal may be considered too risky.

> ■ For example, a certain cosmetics manufacturer waited until it knew the marketing vice-president of its target had left on an extended vacation/overseas business trip before launching a new product line. The organization was paralyzed for several weeks while the stand-in vacillated, unwilling to exercise her authority in the situation for fear of making the wrong move, but reluctant to "contact the boss" for fear of being regarded as "not up to the job."

Finally, answers to the questions presented here should be considered in light of all three behavioral models presented in Chapter 1. Keep in mind that the "rational actor" answers will often require modification due to organizational process or bureaucratic politics interference.

STRATEGIC IMPLICATIONS

As with the management of internal stakeholders, it is critical in the strategy formulation process to identify those external stakeholders who will be affected *most* by or who can *most* affect the strategy, and to formulate political strategies for their management. The format shown in Chapter 4, Table 4.1, can be used with equal success in analyzing external stakeholders' demands and impacts. The political strategist must make every effort to ensure that *all* stakeholders have been identified. Again, careful analysis of the industry chain and potential changes in the infrastructure can do much to bring them to light.

Once all current and potential stakeholders have been identified, analyzed, and their impact studied, political strategies can be formulated to exploit their strengths and weaknesses using the processes outlined in Chapters 2 and 3 and the systematic approach to formulation as discussed in Chapter 7. Before moving on to the formulation process, however, one last topic must be addressed. Chapter 6 integrates the multiple demands placed on the organization by its internal and external stakeholders with a discussion of policy formation as a political process.

SUMMARY: KEY CONCEPTS

1. A large number of major options are available to the strategist when developing a political strategy against target stakeholders. Part of the challenge lies in selecting the correct combination of options from the confusing array available.

2. The first option is selection of target: dependent or competitor. The second option is whether to take direct or indirect action. The third option is whether primarily to manipulate or accommodate. The fourth option is whether to operate within the current system or create a new set of dependents and competitors.

3. Whatever options are selected, it is important to spend some time thinking about the likely responses of the target stakeholder—these responses being to some extent predictable from a careful analysis of the target's strategies, organization, and political systems.

6

Policy Formation as a Political Process

MULTIPLE DEMANDS ON ORGANIZATIONS

■ During the "stagflation" period of the United States economy in the early to the middle seventies, a manufacturer faced the following problems. His bank was calling for him to improve his liquidity, customers were demanding lower prices, his suppliers were asking for earlier payment on his raw materials, his workers were demanding increases in wages, and the shareholders were becoming vociferous about profit improvement and a better dividend payment. The demands this manufacturer faced far exceeded his capacity to meet them, and many of the demands were conflicting. To improve liquidity for the banks required funds, but suppliers wanted these funds to pay for materials. To improve profits required cost cuts or price increases, but labor wanted to raise costs and customers wanted to reduce prices. To increase dividends decreased cash and affected liquidity.

Although this example is drawn from a time when the economy was undergoing exceptional turmoil, it is not unusual in these times of rapid change for organizations to face pressures from their dependents that exceed their capacities to meet them. It is also not unusual for them to manifest conflicts and inconsistencies within themselves. The larger the organization, the more complex these demands become, and soon the capacity of a single manager in the organization to cope with this complexity is completely overwhelmed.

As we mentioned briefly in Chapter 5, the organization's response is to differentiate its structure—to create subparts of the organization to specialize in handling specific relationships with the dependents in the environment (Lawrence and Lorsch 1967).

For instance, a purchasing department will be created to handle raw materials, a personnel department to handle human resources, a financial department to handle funds flow, a products department to handle physical productions, and so on. This specification gives rise to more efficiency, because specialists are given narrower, more comprehensible tasks. Specialization stops the organization from becoming totally paralyzed by the complexity and uncertainty it faces.

For example, a sales manager is in charge of sales. Given the direction to go out and sell, she can go out and push sales without being responsible for whether the raw materials, labor, and products will be there when needed. At the same time, the manufacturing manager can plan the production of products without having to worry about whether they will be sold or whether the labor and materials will be there. The specialized parts of the organization serve the function of absorbing some of the uncertainty for the other parts. At the same time, these parts are insulated from the demands being placed on other parts.

Because it is virtually impossible to make rational decisions in the face of conflicting demands, the organization places a boundary around each aspect of the problem (for example, sales) and gives a person within that boundary the means to make a rational decision without being overly concerned about the conflicting demands and high level of uncertainty that the organization as a whole faces.

However, the very fact that a set of specialized departments is introduced into the organization creates new problems. The people in charge of these functions develop a narrower, more specialized perspective. The sales manager is motivated to seek sales and tends to see everything from a sales point of view. She may consider the production department an irritant, continually complaining about schedule disruptions. The production manager may become obsessed with efficiency of production and see the sales department as an endless source of schedule disruptions.

Out of this specialization (or differentiation) arise multiple goals within the organization—goals that tend to be aligned to the multiple demands flowing in from the dependents. Coupled with the fact that the individuals in charge of divisions, departments, and so on bring to the organization their own sets of aspirations and goals, we have a situation that is rife with potential goal conflicts. (In this text, the subject of goals is treated with a deliberate political perspective. The text by Max Richards, *Setting Strategic Goals and Objectives*, considers goals in more detail and from other perspectives.)

The problem that the differentiated or specialized organization faces is that the narrower perspective created by departmentalization gives rise to interest groups and coalitions within the departments. Individuals in pursuit of their own goals and within their narrower perspective tend to seek others who would like the same goals achieved.

The coalition formation process that was discussed in Chapter 4, coupled with the complexity introduced by the numbers and conflicting demands of external stakeholders that was discussed in Chapter 5, place the organization at the center of multiple, conflicting demands. Some means of resolving the problem has to be developed. Acting within its own political process, the organization must somehow make the difficult resource allocation decisions needed to satisfy these demands.

Since management cannot hope to satisfy all demands simultaneously, it evolves a set of *general policy commitments* that aim to satisfy the majority of demands represented by both internal and external interested stakeholder groups.

THE POLICY FORMATION PROCESS

The process of policy formation is diagrammed in Figure 6.1.

First, look at the left side of the figure. External stakeholders, after due consideration of their alternatives, make demands on the organization. These demands are of two types. *Inducement demands* involve the exchange of the stakeholders' output (for example, labor, price, investment) for a contribution by the organization (salary, product, investment yield). *Policy commitment demands* are for long-term commitment by part of the organization as to the manner in which it will meet certain of these inducement demands. Contracts are one example of policy commitments.

Figure 6.1 Policy Formulation Process

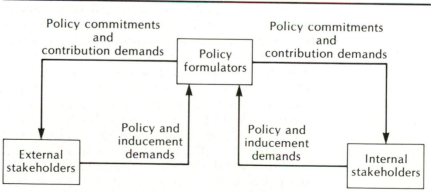

Simultaneously, internal stakeholders (on the right side of the figure) make similar demands on the organization after having considered *their* alternatives.

The leaders of the organization receive these two sets of demands. On the basis of the alternatives available to them, they begin manipulating and accommodating the external and internal stakeholders in an attempt to ensure that the terms of exchange favor the organization (or themselves) as far as possible. They can negotiate with stakeholders by countering their policy and inducement demands with policy commitments and *contribution demands* (the reverse of inducement demands). For illustrative purposes, let us look at the case of a travel company and some of the demands that it faced over a six-month period.

External Stakeholders

The company chartered berths on vessels for sea cruises.

Suppliers: Its major supplier demanded, in addition to the inducement demands relating to charter prices, the following policy commitments: (1) that the company enter into a three-year contract guaranteeing a minimum volume of passengers to each destination and (2) that the company demand from all passengers a 25 percent deposit that would be forwarded immediately to the shipping company.

Banks: The company's major bank wanted the company to commit itself to creating an escrow account in which all customers' prepayments would be deposited to offset a percentage of the current overdraft and specified that the overdraft at no stage exceed a certain level of dollars.

Agents: The company's five major agents, who sold about 40 percent of its volume, were pressing the company to institute a policy that would set aside a guaranteed proportion of berths for each of them for each tour. These were to be released to other agents only after the major agents had had some time to sell these berths.

Internal Stakeholders

Branch Offices: A spokesperson for the branch office managers asked that the branches be paid the same commission as outside agents. (At the time, they received a smaller commission.)

Tour Leaders: Each tour had a leader who represented the company and handled passenger problems. A spokesperson from the tour leaders demanded a "discomfort allowance" for any of the leaders who spent more than a certain number of days per quarter away from home. To date, all employees had been on straight salaries. This was the first demand for a differentiated salary structure.

Marketing Department: Traditionally, the company had spent most of its promotion funds by marketing in the printed media. The marketing department was pressing the company to change over to use of visual and audio media, with a substantial increase in budget.

Policy Decisions

After viewing the alternatives available to each set of stakeholders and to the company, and assessing the relative political capabilities in each case, the company formulated the following policy decisions.

Suppliers: The supplier was an important component in the company's overall strategy and some concessions were made, so the company committed itself to the following policy decisions: (1) that the company would guarantee, via a three-year contract, a minimum volume of dollar business but not by destination and (2) that the company would retain all monies paid in advance by customers.

Bank: That the company would maintain overdraft levels below a certain level of dollars specified by month to take into account cyclicality of sales. (Eventually, the company changed banks.)

Agents: That all agents would have equal access to berth availability, unless agents were prepared to guarantee sales.

Branch Managers: That branch offices would receive the same commission as agents but that they then would pay to the head office a service charge for all expenses incurred by the head office on behalf of the branches, plus a financial fee for head office overhead.

Tour Leaders: That no tour leaders would spend more than a certain number of days per quarter away from home without receiving compensating vacation in another quarter.

Marketing Department: That the promotion budget would remain unchanged but would be used at the discretion of the firm and its marketing department.

After these policies had been negotiated among the various stakeholders, stakeholder support was achieved, and the company proceeded to operate for several years without major changes in these policies.

In developing a political strategy, there is a particularly challenging demand condition that the strategist may face and that is when two or more stakeholders pose irrefutable, conflicting demands.

Irrefutable and Conflicting Demands. Particularly powerful or influential groups inside or outside the organization can make demands that have to be met if their valuable support is to be maintained. These irrefutable demands from key stakeholders constitute the primary constraints on the organization.

Yet, there may be times when demands made on the organization by one group are in conflict with demands made by another group, and the groups making these conflicting demands are sufficiently powerful for the organization to be compelled to try to satisfy them. Three basic strategies can be employed in handling such demands.

Compromise. An attempt can be made to negotiate a compromise between the conflicting groups.

Generalize. We have already argued that when the policy commitments are made sufficiently general, both groups can see some possibility for achieving their specific purposes.

> ■ A company manufacturing electronic instruments was facing decreasing profit margins due to rapidly escalating costs in a tight market. The shareholders were pressing for increased profits, and the workers were becoming increasingly concerned about layoffs and were threatening to unionize if major layoffs took place. Senior management formulated a policy designed to appease demands for more profits and for work force stability by formulating a policy of "increased profitability and growth through more productive use of existing resources." This statement was interpreted by shareholders as a commitment to improving profitability and by the work force as a commitment to maintaining stability of employment. Because the commitment had been phrased in a general way, it obviated specific demands from shareholders to cut costs—notably labor costs—and it obviated specific demands from the work force to guarantee job security.

Thus, generalization of policy commitments is a useful tool for handling conflicting demands from powerful coalitions.

Pay Sequential Attention. If an organization faces a number of demands that are inconsistent with one another, it may be possible to handle this conflict by focusing on one demand at a time while at the same time holding the others in check.

> ■ Consider the case of a production vice-president who was facing demands from customers for better service and quality improvement, demands from his department for increased salaries, and demands from the senior vice-president to reduce escalating costs. The vice-president's tactic was to try to hold quality and delivery at current levels while he improved productivity in the manufacturing plants. He used some of the improvements in productivity to inch up the salaries and wages. As demands from the customers became more insistent, he switched attention from cost reduction and salary improvement, and tried to keep them at

satisfactory levels while he made improvements in quality and delivery to mollify the customers. As the customers began to quiet down, he turned his attention to the cost problem in earnest, since by now management was becoming impatient with the fact that costs were still not declining. Having demonstrated some decline in costs, he could then press for wage and salary improvements in response to the department's complaints that these had been stalled for some time. In this way, he was able to balance a stream of conflicting demands that were, essentially, inconsistent with one another.

Sequential attention to commitments or demands involves paying attention to the demonstration of improvement on one set of demands, while holding the other demands at a level that at least keeps the stakeholders mollified, and then changing attention from the demand on which improvement has been demonstrated to one on which the demands are becoming increasingly insistent. Then, the cycle is repeated. Sequential attention is the only available tool when faced with irrefutable conflicting demands that cannot be compromised.

THE POLICY INTERPRETATION AND EXECUTION PROCESS

Once the policy decisions flowing from the policy formulation process have been accepted by stakeholders, policy execution must take place. It should be remembered that the organization converts inputs from the environment into outputs. This transformation of inputs into outputs must, however, be guided, monitored, and controlled to ensure that the transformations and transactions take place in terms of the formulated policy. The actual detailed and specific sets of small actions that must be carried out to effect this transformation are technical actions, which occur at the technical level of the organization (say the shop floor).

Policy decisions are phrased in broad terms, since they are formulated as general guides to action. They cannot be applied to specific circumstances without interpretation. Therefore, some system of action between the policy formulation level and the technical level is necessary. The functions of this intermediary system are to receive policy decision signals; to interpret these signals for specific situations that arise; in terms of its interpretation of policy, to create specific tasks for the execution of the policies by the technical level; to monitor the performance of the technical level and to adjust action at the level at which action departs from policy; and to mobilize the resources necessary to effect these technical tasks. Parsons (1969) calls these functions of organization the *administrative functions*. To enable such functions to be executed, an intermediate level is created in the organization. The primary function of this level is the interpretation and execution of policy. The organization evolves a hierarchy of administrative offices to perform this task.

The tasks of the incumbents of these offices can be divided into two categories: *mediation* between the organization and the outside to obtain the resources needed to execute policy, and *administration* of the organization's internal affairs to ensure that policy is executed. The nature and flow of interactions between the three organizational levels, and between the levels and their environment, are illustrated in Figure 6.2.

Figure 6.2 **Total Flow of Political Action**

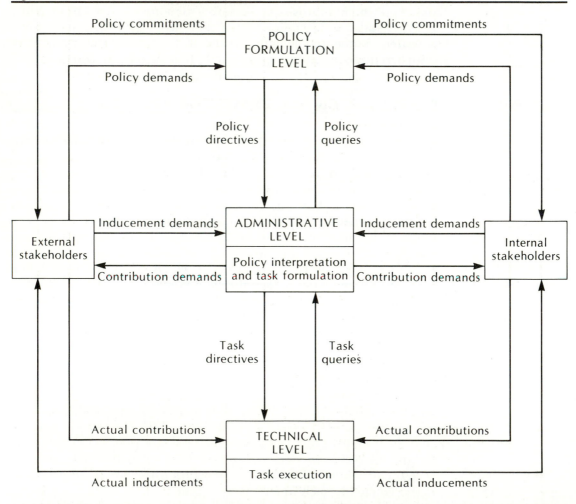

At the administrative level, managers face a variety of inducement demands from both external and internal stakeholders. The managers interpret the policy directives in terms of the specific demands made on them, and then undertake a negotiating process to determine the terms on which inducements will be exchanged for contributions from the external and internal groups. When the terms have been agreed upon, the administrative level generates tasks for the technical level to perform in order to execute the policy. Task directives are transmitted to the technical level.

At the technical level, the actual contributions of the stakeholders are received and converted, according to task directives, into actual inducements that are dispatched to stakeholders.

The administrative level receives two forms of feedback from the technical level. First, task queries are transmitted to the administrative level when situations not covered by the task directives arise. Second, performance is monitored to ensure that the technical level is operating as directed. Similarly, the policy formulation level receives policy queries and managerial/performance feedback.

With this model of political action, the questions that remain to be answered are those concerned with its relevance and application to the formulation of political strategy.

THE RELEVANCE OF POLITICAL ACTION

For these major reasons, the political strategist cannot afford to ignore the political action in organizations in the formulation of political strategy.

First, as we have said before, political strategy is formulated in the context of the strategist's own organization, and internal considerations place constraints on what strategies the formulator is *allowed* to use.

Second, political strategy is formulated in the context of the target organizations; that is to say, the political processes that take place within opposing organizations influence which counterstrategies they will be likely to employ. The astute strategist cannot ignore counterstrategies.

Third, political strategy is concerned with the formation of alliances with other organizations. This alliance is a superorganization in which the same types of political processes as we have described here take place but at an interorganizational level. Such an alliance would be difficult to hold together without an intimate knowledge of the processes that shape and hold it together.

SUMMARY: KEY CONCEPTS

1. Organizations in the act of creating specialized departments also create grounds for potential goal conflicts, since departments tend to develop narrow specialized perspectives.

2. Policy commitments must be formulated to satisfy the demands of powerful internal and external interest groups.

3. In the cases in which these policy demands by interest groups are in conflict, three forms of response are available: compromise, generalization of policy commitments, and sequential attention to commitments.

4. The astute leader of a complex organization should be able to cope with the conflicting sets of demands facing her and recognize that it is only via management of the organizational political processes that a viable, adaptable organization can be maintained. It is through the political processes that disparate, but important, environmental demands are articulated.

5. Understanding political processes in organizations helps the political strategist to (a) avoid strategies that will not be accepted by his own organization; (b) anticipate responses that stakeholders may make to his strategies; (c) identify the policies and commitments that limit the stakeholders' actions; and (d) control the interorganizational coalitions of alliances he may form.

7

Political Strategy Formulation

In this chapter, the principles of political strategy formulation are laid out. The next four chapters provide illustration of these principles with detailed case examples. The framework developed in this chapter and shown in operation in the cases that follow integrates the material presented in the preceding chapters. This framework suggests four main phases of political strategy formulation:

1. Analysis of the total situation
2. Identification of future threats and opportunities
3. Political analysis
4. Political strategy formulation

Table 7.1 summarizes the steps involved in each of the four phases. Since the first two phases are essentially the same as those of Hofer and Schendel (1978) in this series, the discussion of these phases is brief. We concentrate instead on the last two.

ANALYSIS OF THE TOTAL SITUATION

Preliminary Analysis

The analysis of the total situation begins with a specification of the firm as a system interacting with its environment. A systematic identification of all the people, groups, or organizations on which the firm depends for its inputs is made. At the same time, the major competitors for these inputs are also identified. Note that for political strategy formulation, this analysis has a wider scope than is

Table 7.1   Four Phases of Political Strategy Formulation

1. Analysis of the total situation
   — Preliminary analysis
   — Trend analysis and forecasting

2. Identification of future threats and opportunities
   — Critical threats to survival
   — Outstanding opportunities open to the firm
   — Potential allies in each critical decision area
   — Potential opponents in each critical decision area

3. Political analysis
   — External political capability
      — Nature of relationships
      — Power and influence resources
      — External coalition structure
   — Internal political structure
      — Strategy
      — Organizational processes
      — Political structure
   — Strengths and weaknesses
   — Impact of economic strategy
      — Major stakeholder groups
      — Coalition formation

4. Political strategy formulation
   — Establishing independent capability
   — Alliance selection
   — Alliance negotiation
   — Offensive and defensive strategies

normal for economic strategy formulation. Thus, instead of concentrating on a customer/market/product analysis, such stakeholders as shareholders, employee groups, unions, competitors, and suppliers should also be analyzed and then examined for their possible impact on the economic strategy.

Trend Analysis and Forecasting

Essentially, the same type of trend analysis as are discussed in Hofer and Schendel (1978) should be carried out at three levels: the international/national level, the industry level, and the organizational level. However, in addition to identifying the trends associated with the firm itself, it is also important to identify trends associated with any of the major stakeholders identified in the systems analysis discussed previously.

The implications of the prior analyses are overlaid on the firm's current position. The object is to gain insight into how and where the firm depends most on its environment and what trends in these dependencies are likely to occur. An analysis of these trends in relation to the firm's activities will indicate where the future threats to the firm's survival and outstanding opportunities for its future might lie. Let us term these *critical decision areas.*

IDENTIFICATION OF FUTURE THREATS AND OPPORTUNITIES

A political approach argues that the firm should actively maneuver to promote its own goals. It is pointless for the firm to strive toward these goals on its own if there are allies willing and able to help it. These allies are found by identifying who else is going to be affected by the threats and opportunities identified. Any actor who is likely to be negatively affected by the threats is a potential ally. Any actor who is likely to benefit from the opportunities is a potential ally.

On the other hand, the actors who will suffer if the opportunity is seized by the firm form the potential opposition. Actors posing critical threats, or those who stand to benefit from these threats, are also potential opposition.

From the above analyses the following should emerge.

1. The critical threats to survival
2. The outstanding opportunities open to the firm
3. The potential allies in each critical decision area
4. The potential opposition in each critical decision area

POLITICAL ANALYSIS

A political analysis aims at identifying the political capabilities (power and influence) of the key actors in the situation.

The object of such a political analysis is to determine, for each potential ally or opponent, where it is dependent on its environment; for the more one can gain control of these dependencies, the more one can gain control of the actions of the relevant players. At the same time, the dependencies of the firm should be identified so that action can be taken to block similar maneuvers by the opposition.

In the following discussion of the process of political analysis, only the broad theme of the analysis will be outlined, since the detailed considerations have been discussed earlier in the book and will be applied in the cases that follow.

External Political Capability

The first step in the political analysis involves determining the power and influence bases of the various players. Here, the application of the material in Chapter 2 is required.

Nature of the Relationship between the Players and Their Environment. A relationship analysis is done to determine what dependencies exist between the player and its environment. We use the term *player* rather than *organization*, because the target can be an individual, unit, department, or firm. In every case, the issues for analysis are the same—only the scope will differ. The player's alternative structure should also be explored: For which goods and services is it dependent and on whom is it dependent?

Power and Influence Resources. By analyzing the dependencies of each critical player, we can get a sense of the strategic power and influence resources that will determine the behavior of the critical player. Areas of high dependency where there are few alternatives or where the marginal impact of single alternatives is high are important. Resources that could become critical in the future should be identified. Areas where the critical player has high commitment should be identified. Areas where the critical player has audience and possesses strategic information are indicators of the player's influence base. Finally, areas where the player has formal authority should be identified.

External Coalition Structure. It is also important to get a sense of what interorganizational coalitions the critical player has joined and what issues gave rise to these coalitions. A change in the visibility or priority of these issues may disrupt the coalition.

A similar analysis should be carried out for the firm formulating the strategy itself. Once this type of analysis has been done, it is appropriate to do an *internal* analysis of the critical player.

Internal Political Structure

Strategy, Objectives, and Long-Range Resources Commitments. As we saw in Chapter 5, strategy analysis gives us a sense of what constrains the organization's capacity to redirect its efforts and of what it considers to be important and worth fighting for. It also provides the basis for rationalizing any major moves it will be making.

Organizational Processes. Analysis of organizational processes provides us with insights into the perspective from which various key decision makers within the organization view their environment and the shifts in that environment. It also gives us a sense of the rate at which the organization will respond to change, the amount of disruption such change could cause, the patterns of responses that could emerge from such change, and the level in the organization at which changes will be addressed.

Political Structure.   Here we are interested in what demands major external and internal interest groups are making of the critical player, who the dominant coalition members are, what major policy commitments have been made, and how and at what level discretion is employed and constrained by the politics of the system.

In our initial analysis, at least, many gaps in the information we desire will occur. Often it will be necessary to go without much of the previous information, but it has been found that much of this information is available from members of our own organization once the specific questions are asked, or is available with a little effort, from other interested organizations.

Strengths and Weaknesses

The political systems of the critical players are now analyzed to determine their strengths and weaknesses. This analysis should reveal whether they are highly dependent on parts of their environment, whether their internal political system is strained by internal conflict, whether their key personnel are dissatisfied with the ideology of the system, whether the structure of the system is so cumbersome that they cannot respond quickly to political maneuvering, whether their resources are at present immobilized by heavy commitments to others, and so on. Usually, a small number of important strengths and weaknesses of the critical players are identified.

If interesting dependencies are identified, it may be worthwhile to carry the analysis even further and analyze the systems on which the critical player is dependent. This type of information will often provide an indication of where indirect political action is possible.

The idea is not to become entangled in a vast web of detailed and complex analyses but to start at a broad level, try to identify important factors, and then pursue these factors in more detail.

Impact of Economic Strategy

By following the guidelines set by Hofer (1986), the firm will have developed an economic strategy aimed at securing a strong position in the marketplace. *It cannot be stressed too strongly that the fundamental basis of long-run survival lies in a sound economic strategy,* which is the reason for the firm's very existence in society. The purpose, then, of the political strategy is to enhance and complement the economic strategy allowing for successful implementation.

Use of the guidelines proposed by Hofer will identify the specific strengths and weaknesses of the firm in an economic market context. From this process will emerge the strategic decisions as to which opportunities and threats must be addressed by the firm in order for it to survive and prosper in the marketplace.

In this book we are not concerned with how these decisions are made. The opportunities and threats to be addressed are taken as given, and we proceed from the political analysis, assuming that the economic strategy has been determined. We proceed with political strategy formulation by asking how the environment is to be restructured in such a way that the success of the economic strategy is assured.

There is, however, one major caveat that is of relevance in this book. The proposed economic strategy must be assessed in terms of the internal political systems of the firm proposing it. The concepts developed in Chapters 4 and 6 should therefore be applied to determine how the proposed economic strategy is going to integrate with the political processes of the firm. If the optimal economic strategy lacks internal support, it may be wiser to select a different but still viable strategy. To help determine whether a proposed strategy is organizationally viable, the strategist should focus on the following issues.

Major Stakeholder Groups. A strategy cannot be successful without a high degree of commitment inside the organization. It is inevitable that any major organizational changes are going to benefit some parts of the organization to the detriment of others. The strategist should be aware of which changes are which and get a sense of where resistance to the strategy will be experienced. The strategist must then decide what must be done to ensure that the correct degree of commitment is obtained in the organization.

Coalition Formation. Strategic decisions raise issues in the organization, which in turn will give rise to coalitions structured around these issues. The strategist should attempt to determine beforehand what coalitions will form and what the power and influence bases of these coalitions are. If this activity is not managed, the entire strategy could be subverted or at least redirected. A prior estimate of the issues that are likely to arise and the power and influence of the coalitions that are likely to form gives the strategist the necessary foresight to adapt beforehand to the expected conditions.

The strategist can prepare for this in several ways (again, see Chapters 4 and 6): by adjusting the authority structure in subtle ways to reduce the power and influence of certain members, by formulating ahead of time the kinds of generalized policy commitments that will be necessary to obtain broader support, by determining ahead of time what sequential attention patterns will be necessary to maintain support as the strategy is launched and implemented, or by deciding what issues to make visible and what priorities to set on these issues, so that the strategist can control some of the coalition formation in the organization. The larger and more complex the organization, the more important it is that these factors be given consideration.

If the strategy being contemplated runs a high risk of being subverted by internal dissension, then it is inappropriate, however attractive it may be when viewed in an external context. The first actions to be taken, then, should be those that will make it internally appropriate. We do not need to have *total* commitment, but we do need to have sufficient internal commitment for success. Often, parts of the organization will be dissatisfied with the strategy. We must ensure that they do not endanger the strategy by their lack of commitment.

Assuming that a strategy has been evolved in which the internal commitment is adequate, it is then possible to proceed with the formulation of political strategy.

POLITICAL STRATEGY FORMULATION

Establishing Independent Capability

As a first step, the strengths and weaknesses of the firm and its opposition should be matched against one another to determine, roughly, the firm's political capability vis-à-vis its opposition. From this matching process, the firm obtains a general idea of its capacity to cope with the critical decision areas independent of its allies. An assessment of what the firm can do *without* allies lays the groundwork for clearly determining the bargaining base in future negotiations with potential allies.

Alliance Selection

Knowing its capacity to cope with a situation on its own, the firm is now in a position to set tentative objectives with respect to the best position that it can hope to reach by acting independently against the opposition. These tentative objectives form the basis of the firm's decisions on the selection of allies. Since the independent political capability of the firm itself constitutes the "bargaining base" of the firm in subsequent negotiations with allies, it will accept no agreement with allies that will cause it to achieve less than it would by acting on its own (see Chapter 3).

For the next step, the firm must select a combination of allies for each critical decision area. The combined strengths and weaknesses of the final alliance must be matched against the strengths and weaknesses of the opposition. The problem is that the firm must cope with a whole set of critical decision areas. An ally that is useful in one critical decision area may prove incompatible with another area. The firm's problem is to determine the best set of allies for its total strategy. This determination should be made by means of a cyclical procedure. A combination of allies is selected, and the compatibility with the firm's objectives is assessed. If they are compatible, the firm assesses first the extent to which the alliance it forms for each critical decision area can cope with those of the opposition in that critical decision and, second, the extent to which the firm itself can cope with the alliance.

Since goals of the firm and its allies will not be perfectly congruent, the firm should identify and list the major issues that will arise in the alliance if it is formed. If these issues will cause insurmountable incompatibilities between the firm and a potential ally, that ally is disqualified. After a few alternative alliances have been considered, a best alliance can usually be selected.

In the next step, the firm must negotiate with the potential allies to form the alliance. At this stage, the firm should consider the options at its disposal. Depending on the structures of dependents or competitors in the situation, the firm should review the options available, and undertake political action to ensure that the best conditions prevail for itself before it enters alliance formation.

The firm then undertakes political action directed toward the potential allies, attempting to structure the conditions so that the agreements reached with alliance members will turn out best for both parties. Since it *wants* to reach agreement with the allies, it can ill afford to alienate them. Alliance negotiation therefore involves maintaining a delicate balance between achieving as much for the firm as possible but not endangering the alliance by being greedy. The major manipulative tools at this stage tend to be persuasion and inducement rather than coercion and obligation. The win-win strategies discussed in Chapter 3 is the preferred approach.

Alliance Negotiations

For negotiations that are critical to the strategic future of the firm, a well-prepared negotiating strategy is essential. Here, the concepts and tactics developed in Chapter 3 should be applied. The most important are the following:

Identification of Major Negotiation Issues That Will Arise, accompanied by an analysis of the stand to be taken on these issues, in terms of the priority of such issues for the firm and the estimated priority for its targets.

Identification of Critical Issues and the key bluffs, threats, and promises that the firm will use or expect the target to use.

Specification of Desired Agenda, which should be structured in such a way that differences in issue priorities can be used to advantage.

Information Gathering about the potential allies, particularly concerning their previous tactics, the context in which they make decisions, the alternatives they have, and who their key decision makers are.

Identification of Critical Stages at which the process may need reassessment as missing information about the opponents is obtained.

Development of a Negotiating Theme, which will be used to tie the arguments together and support the key bluffs, threats, and promises required in handling the issues.

Establishment of Checkpoints and Objectives by which the firms's negotiators can assess their performance as each stage of the negotiation is concluded.

Identification of Implementation Issues, which must be addressed *before* the firm launches the strategy, so that implementation is rapid and effective.

The firm should then negotiate an alliance and, subject to the results of this negotiation, reset its tentative objectives. It can now begin to develop the political strategies that it and the alliance will bring to bear against the opposition.

Offensive and Defensive Strategies

With the formation of the alliance, new information regarding the strengths and weaknesses of the allies and the opposition may be brought in, and it may be necessary to modify the firm's original assessments of the alliance's strengths and weaknesses.

The alliance can now develop an offensive strategy (1) to exploit the opposition's weaknesses and (2) to erode the opposition's strengths. It simultaneously develops a defensive strategy for countering the opposition's attempts (1) to exploit the alliance's weaknesses and (2) to erode the alliance's strengths.

If, as is usual, the opposition is strong, then inevitably the alliance will have to negotiate with them. In this case, the alliance should first attempt to manipulate the situation by using the power and influence at its disposal, and then to accommodate by bargaining. This sequencing must be taken into account when strategies are being formulated.

In formulating the offensive and defensive strategies, the strategist must bear in mind these points:

1. Action should be arranged when the strategist's strategic resources are as high as possible and the opponent's are as low as possible. This factor could necessitate delaying action until the time is right.
2. The strategist should build a solid knowledge of the key decision makers in the opposition. It is important to remember that ultimately, the opposition's responses are the results of decisions made by people. Therefore, once the general focus of the political strategy has been determined, the strategist needs to know how the key people in the situation will be affected.
3. A strategy is not unilateral. The opposition can be expected to respond. The rational actor, organizational process, and political models presented in Chapter 1 should be used to develop and anticipate the strategic responses of the opposition.

Once the strategies have been formulated, detailed plans may be developed and monitoring systems put in place to evaluate the effectiveness of these plans. Once the political strategy is initiated, it must be monitored and updated as time progresses. The results of this monitoring process constitute the triggers and inputs for any necessary changes in the strategy. Practical applications of the concepts and processes presented in this chapter are illustrated in four cases that follow in Chapters 8, 9, 10, and 11.

Each case has been selected because it highlights specific facets of the political strategy process. No one case makes use of all the concepts in this book. It is impossible, even in four cases, to illustrate all the concepts discussed; however, they have all proved useful at one time or another.

Before the illustrative cases are discussed, some caveats and qualifications are given:

1. In the illustrative cases that follow, space limitations demand that a simplified situation be described. The purpose of the cases is to illustrate, not to provide a complete case history. The cases attempt to convey the key concepts in developing a political strategy.

2. It so happens that the first case involves national politics. This need not have been the case. The activities of the firm are political in the sense defined in the prior chapters and not in the national political sense, as we shall see in the next two cases. What the first case does underline, however, is that the concepts of political strategy developed in this book *do* have applications up to the level of national politics.

3. Please note that in not one of the cases does the company involved formulate a political strategy that is in direct conflict with the public interest. Political strategy can (and should) be employed in ways that do not involve illegal or immoral activities.

4. In the interest of keeping the confidence of the companies who have participated in the development of this book, their names, products, or countries (or a combination of these) have been disguised. The cases and examples in this book are illustrative, and one should not make assumptions based on similarities that one sees between the case material and specific companies.

FINAL COMMENTS

Before we move on to the cases, however, a few final comments are in order. First, a political approach to strategy formulation captures the essence of what is largely ignored yet appears to be an overriding concern of many senior managers observed in practice. The political approach provides a framework for addressing the aggressive, competitive strategic action that characterizes many dynamic business environments today. It lays the theoretical groundwork for explaining the action that aggressive managers intuitively develop in the pursuit of their corporate goals.

Second, this introductory text merely provides an overview of the subject of organizational politics. A great deal remains to be explored and explained. Much work is already being carried out by social scientists in many different types of organizations. The thoughts and insights these social scientists are providing are particularly applicable to the field of management. Much more research can be done directly in the field of organizational politics to give more substance to the strategic decision-making process.

Third, the approach raises a need for case studies and organizational analyses that focus on the practical application of the concepts in this book to strategic situations, both in practice and for teaching purposes.

Fourth, and by no means least important, the subject matter treated in this book raises questions relating to ethics. What needs to be explored and thought through by readers is what the limits to ethical behavior are in applying the concepts herein. We stated in the first chapter that the principles in this book can be applied within the ethical constraints of individual readers but readers themselves must identify their own constraints on behavior to best determine what actions constitute compromise.

8

Illustrative Case Study:
Alpha Oil Mills

THE SITUATION

Alpha Oil Mills, a producer of edible oils, has identified a major strategic opportunity: the manufacture of margarine.[1] Alpha, however, is located in an agricultural country that suffered severely during the depression years, during which the powerful dairy farm lobby in the government succeeded in prohibiting the sale of butter substitutes: Margarine sales are prohibited by legislation. Dairy product sales are carefully monitored by a dairy control board—a semiautonomous government body instituted to protect the interests of the dairy farmers. Alpha, however, is intent on manufacturing margarine because it has tremendous potential.

Alpha is part of the oilseed-processing industry (Figure 8.1). This industry in general obtains oilseed from oilseed farmers (1), via an oilseed control board (2), another semiautonomous government body instituted to protect the interests of the oilseed farmers. The oilseeds are processed in different ways to form cooking oils and fats, which are sold (3) to consumers (the distribution system is ignored for the example).

Meal, a by-product of the oil-recovery process, is made into ani mal feeds and sold (4) to meat producers, egg producers, and dairy farmers. Butter is produced by dairy farmers and channeled (6) via the auspices of the dairy control board to dairies (7) and then to the final consumer (8).

---

1. The Alpha Oil Mills case has been briefly discussed in a previous publication (MacMillan 1972).

111

Figure 8.1   Initial Analysis of the Oilseed Industry

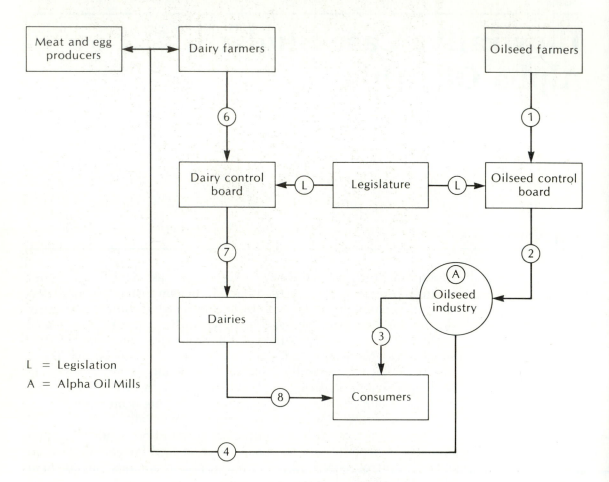

L = Legislation
A = Alpha Oil Mills

Source: I. C. MacMillan, "Business Strategies for Political Action," *Journal of General Management* 2(1) (Autumn 1974). Reprinted by permission.

The critical stakeholders that Alpha identified are the competitors, the consumers, the dairy farmers, the dairy control board, the meat and egg producers, the oilseed control board, and the oilseed farmers.

Potential allies include the competitors and the consumers who would all benefit by the introduction of margarine. Potential targets are the dairy farmers and the dairy control board.

POLITICAL ANALYSIS OF THE ALPHA OIL MILLS SYSTEM

With the results of an expanded external political system analysis overlaid on the initial industry analysis, a diagram such as Figure 8.2 is obtained.

Figure 8.2 *Expanded Analysis of the Oilseed Industry*

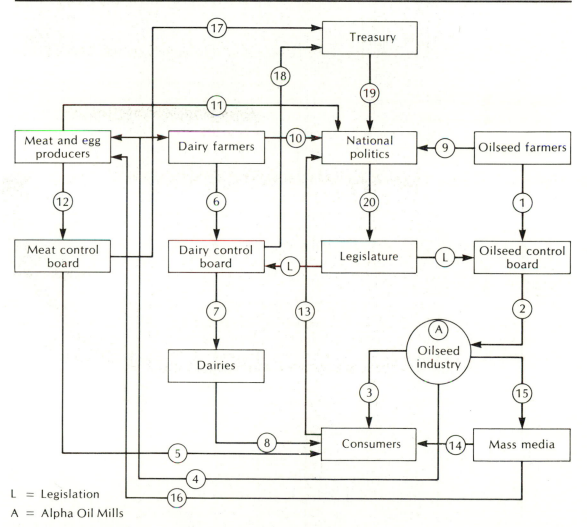

L = Legislation
A = Alpha Oil Mills

Source: I. C. MacMillan, "Business Strategies for Political Action," *Journal of General Management* 2(1) (Autumn 1974). Reprinted by permission.

In the example, the most important relations are the following. The oilseed farmers are a significant lobbying group in national politics (9), as are the dairy farmers (10) and the meat and egg producers (11). Meat and egg producers supply their products (12) to the same type of control boards as the dairy and oilseed industries. The meat and egg control boards distribute the products to consumers (5). The consumers' attitudes play a role in national politics (13). These attitudes are influenced by mass media (14), which could possibly be used by the oilseed industry (15) to influence consumers and the meat and egg producers (16). In addition to internal sales, the control boards are responsible for exporting their constituents' products (or importing them in times of shortage). Its activities are closely observed by the treasury (17 and 18), which is concerned with problems of balance of payments.

Efficient and low-cost meat and egg production is essential if the country is to compete in world export markets. If meat production costs can be reduced, consumers will be satisfied and export prices will be more acceptable to world markets. The treasury will gain valuable foreign revenue if meat exports can be increased.

Butter shortages cause butter imports, which in turn cause increased foreign expenditure (18), an anathema to the treasury, which has a significant say in national politics (19). National politics results in legislation (20).

One way to reduce meat and egg costs is for producers to enter industrialized farming. This necessitates the use of animal feeds, but the problem with animal feeds is that they are expensive. The profits from sales of edible oil and cooking fat are relatively low. With minimal additional investment, Alpha could produce large quantities of margarine at a price substantially below that of butter and still make good profits. As things stand, they have to maintain high feed prices, because the profits on oil and fats are depressed.

If the restriction on margarine could be removed or relaxed, some of the profits of margarine production could be diverted to paying higher prices for oilseeds on the one hand and charging lower prices for feed meals on the other. However, this process is being impeded by the dairy control board, acting under the regulations imposed by the dairy control bill.

As a result of the political analysis, more potential allies have been identified. The potential allies of Alpha now include the other oilseed processors, the oilseed control board, the oilseed farmers, the meat and egg control boards, the meat and egg producers, and the treasury.

ANALYSIS OF THE STRENGTHS
AND WEAKNESSES OF THE OPPOSITION

Strengths of Opposition

The major strength of the opposition is that the dairy control board is a semiautonomous body that has full authority regarding sales of all dairy products and their substitutes. Its autonomy is protected by legislation, which can be changed only through an extremely lengthy (and frustrating) process.

The other major strength is the significant lobbying power of the farmers in national politics, who usually support one another en masse. However, by refocusing on issues of oilseed and meal prices, it may be possible to divide the farmers into two opposing coalitions: dairy farmers versus egg, meat, and oilseed farmers.

Weaknesses of Opposition

Butter production is highly dependent on climatic conditions. In years of drought, butter demand exceeds supply, and butter has to be imported at great cost, causing a drain on foreign currency reserves. The treasury would prefer this not to happen. In these periods, butter prices increase substantially, which is hard on the consumers.

Butter production costs are high, and butter is expensive. Many sectors of the general public would prefer to have margarine.

In years of drought, demand for animal feeds increases.

Alpha is virtually powerless on its own. It needs the support of the entire edible-oil industry if the situation is to be changed. Therefore, it cannot set tentative objectives for acting independently. It can, however, set the constraint that it get at least a fair share of what any alliance accomplishes.

It is compelled to resort to the use of allies, so the strengths and weaknesses of the potential allies must be identified.

POTENTIAL ALLIES

Strengths of Potential Allies

1. Margarine is cheaper than butter, which will mean that if the consumers as a group could be politically activated, a great deal of pressure could be exerted on the national political structure. This strategy will require the support of the media.

2. Meat and egg producers would have a significant lobbying power in national politics if they could be politically activated.

3. Oilseed farmers would have a significant lobbying power if they could be politically activated.

4. The other control boards have leverage that they could use against the dairy control board.

Weaknesses of Potential Allies

1. Consumers are politically apathetic.

2. The oilseed processors have little lobbying power in national politics.

3. Politically motivating the other potential allies may be difficult.

Alliance Strategy

The firm should obviously ally itself with other oilseed producers to present a united front to other key stakeholders. However, with limited lobbying power, it is unlikely that such an alliance will accomplish much more than the firm alone. Therefore, a broader alliance must be sought.

It is unlikely that the oilseed farmers and consumers can be activated without extensive persuasive efforts. If they are to be activated, the media must be brought in. The meat producers may be interested in lobbying for margarine products if this means that cheaper feeds will be available.

The first tentative combination of allies may then be oilseed producers, the oilseed control board, meat and egg producers, and the mass media. In such an alliance, the following major issues will arise.

1. The major issue for the oil processors will be the market share split.

2. The major issue for the meat and egg producers will be the animal feed prices.

3. The major issue for the oilseed control board and the oilseed farmers will be the price they receive for seed.

4. The major issue for the mass media will be that the consumer gets a fair deal in butter and margarine pricing.

On the basis of its assessment of the alliance's chances of success, the firm now estimates the extent to which its objectives should be redefined.

It might decide that in the course of time, it can aim for relaxation of the total restrictions on margarine to allow X tons of production per year and that it will be able to capture Y percent of the market. Since the support that the alliance obtains from the meat and egg producers is more important than the profits obtained from feeds, it could decide that a reduced feed price should be offered as an inducement for support.

In this case, the set of allies was fairly obvious. In more complex cases, it will not be so, since a complete set of critical decision areas, not just one, would be dealt with, and a potential ally in one area may be incompatible in another.

The firm now starts manipulating to set up the alliance. The firm needs to approach its competitors with the idea of presenting a united front to two major groups: the oilseed control board and the meat and egg control boards. The idea would be to "threaten," in an indirect way, that seed prices must come down and that feed prices must go up. With a united front, this threat can be made persuasively. Objections from the boards would be met with the "explanation" that the situation is not like that in other countries where all parties benefit from the large profits reaped from margarine manufacture. The delicate part consists of persuading competitors to go along with the "threat," ensuring that the firm gets a fair share of the end result.

Once a tentative alliance with the boards is established, the media can be appraised of the "conflict" that is taking place, where the emphasis would be (1) on the high cost of butter compared with the cost of margarine for the consumer media, (2) the reasons for the high cost of feeds, and (3) the reasons for the low price of seeds in the agricultural press.

Once this alliance has formed, the offensive and defensive strategies can be developed.

OFFENSIVE AND DEFENSIVE STRATEGIES

Offensive Strategy

Exploitation of Opposition's Weaknesses. The major weaknesses of the opposition arise from the fact that butter must be imported at increased prices in times of drought and that butter is expensive. This weakness can be exploited during a drought when butter has to be imported (necessitating expenditure of foreign resources) and when all the livestock farmers (including the dairy farmers!) are obliged to buy feeds at higher prices at a time they can least afford it.

Erosion of Opposition's Strengths. The major strength of the opposition lies in the autonomy of the dairy control board. This strength can be eroded by creation of pressures on several fronts to alter the legislation protecting the control board.

Defensive Strategy

Covering of Alliance's Weaknesses. The major weakness of the alliance is the apathy of the consumers. The interest of consumer groups must be aroused by mass media publicity when butter imports start coming in or when a price increase is suggested. The high price of meat as a result of the cost of feeds can also be brought to their attention.

Preventing Erosion of Alliance's Strengths. The strengths of the alliance are least effective in times of good rainfall, when there are no imports and prices of butter and feeds are coming down.

The essence of the timing of strategy emerges here. It may take many years to implement a strategy when legislation has to be changed. There are times in this period when odds are in the favor of the opposition and times when the alliance has the upper hand.

The focus of the strategy is also important. Nothing can be done until legislation has been changed. The decision makers are located in the legislature, and the final focus should be there. An understanding of the process whereby legislative decisions are made is therefore necessary.

To summarize briefly, legislators are pressured by constituents to enact legislation. Powerful and influential constituents channel demands from the political "market" to legislators, who try to formulate policy to handle these demands. In so doing, they touch bases with the administrative or executive functions of the government.

In this situation, Alpha and the alliance must create the pressures on the legislators and ensure strong support for these pressures from the administration.

The final strategy, therefore, is to attack whenever there are periods of drought, particularly when these periods are accompanied by low foreign exchange reserves and balance of payment difficulties. This attack should take place at three levels. First, the consumer public should be activated via consumer group and media action, and the agricultural public should be activated via the agricultural press. This tactic is not particularly difficult, since those media take seriously their role as guardians of their constituents' interests. This political activation will give rise to pressures on legislators.

Second, the key influencers in the farm lobby should be identified. These are usually a relatively small number of opinion leaders in each farming community, and particular attention should be focused in areas where extensive egg, meat, and oilseed production takes place. Such opinion leaders may also be members of the legislature!

Third, the key administrators in the executive body should be identified. In this case treasury officials and meat, oilseed, and egg control board officials are held responsible for the execution of legislative policy, and are the targets of the public ire when the public is aroused.

The strategy, then, would be to wait for periods of drought or low reserves of foreign exchange (or both) and then "push" prices on feeds as hard as possible, to depress prices for oilseeds as low as possible and, via the media, to ensure that every butter import and every increase in butter price are made dramatically visible.

At the same time, the sales staffs of the oilseed producers should be relaying the reasons for high feed prices to the opinion leaders (who, incidentally, are often the biggest buyers) in the meat and egg farming community. Finally, the purchasing staff should be active among the opinion leaders of the oilseed farming community.

If the attack is repeated every time a drought condition occurs, the strengths of the opposition will erode as the dairy board and the dairy control bill supporters come under fire in situations in which they are least able to justify themselves. Eventually, the board will be forced to negotiate concessions.

And it is here that the final nuances of a well-conceived political strategy are played out. First, Alpha and its allies must recognize the vast difference between legislation that completely prohibits margarine production and legislation that simply restricts margarine production. In the second case, the thin edge of the wedge that will break the whole structure is in place, and it is vitally important to recognize that the initial negotiation to relax prohibition is but part of a longer-term goal. Probably the best they should shoot for is import replacement, subject to being allowed to produce the same amount in nondrought years. Later strategy can be devoted to improving this position.

Second, Alpha should recognize that the negotiation will create two major opportunities: one to stabilize the industry by indirect accommodation and the other to establish a high price for the margarine. It must be recognized that the dairy board will come to the negotiating table with the express purpose of defending the interests of the dairy industry. They will, therefore, make strong demands to hold the price of margarine at levels that will not make the difference between butter and margarine too large, and will demand guarantees that margarine producers will comply with quotas. Then, the oilseed processors can all be "forced" to commit themselves to a high pricing structure and market-sharing agreement that will be legally sanctioned, all the while steadfastly arguing for a lower price and freedom of market.

CONCLUSION

We have presented a broad-brush analysis of the Alpha Oil Mills case. The purpose here was to overview the development of political strategy using the process outlined in Chapter 7. In the next case (A. Bailey), we focus in more detail on another set of concepts—the concepts of strategic anticipation, analysis of key decision makers, and analysis of a threat and an opportunity.

9

Illustrative Case Study:
A. Bailey (Pty), Ltd.

BACKGROUND

A. Bailey (Pty), Ltd., an equipment company, has been in existence for nearly thirty years.[1] It was started by an Englishman, Alan Bailey, a civil engineer who had been employed in his native land by a firm of consultants specializing in sewage treatment. His work brought him into contact with a firm of equipment suppliers, and hearing that they were looking for a salesperson in Australia, he volunteered his sevices.

Alan Bailey was soon on his way to Sydney, where he made contact with a couple of ex-university friends who had immigrated before the war and who now had some seniority in a local firm of consulting civil engineers. Within weeks of his arrival, Alan had his first order. Being something of an opportunist, he wrote to his employers, handing in his notice but asking to be allowed to remain an independent local agent for all the British company's products and enclosing a copy of the order. Much to Bailey's surprise, his terms were accepted, and he registered the company as A. Bailey (Pty), Ltd., sewage engineers.

In spite of Bailey's initial success, the first ten years were not easy. Money was always short, and strange things sometimes happened to his equipment. At certain times of the year, the whole process would suddenly "invert," and instead of the solid matter in the sewage settling in the tanks while the clear liquid decanted off, the reverse would happen.

---

1. The authors wish to thank R. W. Batson for his assistance in developing this case in its original form.

Bailey gradually modified his equipment to combat this and other local problems arising from differences in diet and high temperatures. He added bits of equipment from other manufacturers to his range and employed a biochemist to sort out his process problems.

By the mid sixties, A. Bailey (Pty), Ltd., held over 60 percent of the market and was considered the expert in sewage in the country. Its customers were almost entirely municipalities, where the engineers tended to be extremely conservative in outlook, preferring to deal with people and equipment that were well tried and tested.

ADVENT OF COMPETITON

Bailey's problems started when people in the Western world began to worry seriously about pollution. In the late seventies, pollution became the "in" word, and many companies (busy with their strategic planning) realized that here was an area where large sums of money would soon be spent by industrialists and municipalities forced by the sheer weight of public opinion to clear up their effluents. Millions of dollars, pounds, and francs were spent by these companies in developing processes, equipment, and techniques to combat pollution, and millions more were spent trying to persuade the industrialists and local authorities to buy them—generally without much success. To spread their increasing overheads, Western manufacturers decided to widen their markets and "discovered" Australia.

Armed with new processes, new equipment, and marginal costing, they invaded the quiet sanctuaries of city engineers' departments and demanded to be heard. No one wanted to listen. After all, the fact that a sewage plant might work in Brussels did not mean it would work in Broken Hill.

"Sure," said the competitors, "but instead of taking you to Adelaide to see a sewage plant, we will take you to Fontainebleau and then on to Paris and Hamburg and Stockholm and London." Visibly affected by the sudden technical advantages of this new process, many engineers modified their conservative attitudes. On the new equipment supplied, however, the sewage inverted in the tanks. This was a case of start-up problems. However, many new plants were still having sporadic "start-up" problems after two years of service.

At the time of the case, A. Bailey (Pty), Ltd., has 20 percent of the market. Alan is old, tired, and ready to hand over the business to his son, Jeff.

THE SITUATION AS JEFF BAILEY SEES IT

National Trends

Australia is becoming increasingly aware of the dangers of pollution and the shortage of water. Domestic effluent is being treated and recycled in western Australia. The Ministry of Water Affairs is setting even stricter standards for effluents. Untreated sewage may not be discharged directly in the sea. Industrial effluents are being checked. Conferences are being held in Sydney, Melbourne, and Perth on how to control pollution.

The population is growing and shifting to the towns, increasing the loads on existing sewage plants. Increasing immigration adds to this load. Currently, about 70 percent of the sewage equipment market is in large towns or cities, and the balance is in small towns in more remote districts.

Trends in the Industry

The total amount of money spent per year for the treatment of liquid effluents will increase substantially due to:

1. increases in population and industrial activity.
2. increases in strictness of legislation.
3. increased public awareness of the damages of pollution.

Where groups of towns form into metropolitan areas, there could be a tendency to combine sewage flows and to treat the effluent in one super treatment works that requires less labor to run and is more resistant to "poisoning" by sudden surges of industrial effluent.

Chemical (as opposed to biological) treatment will come into favor, either on its own or as a tertiary stage, to bring the final effluent up to drinking-water standards.

Trace elements (dissolved inorganics that are present in small quantities) are presently ignored but will increase in concentration as intentional or unintentional recycling occurs. In the United States, certain authorities are beginning to appreciate the dangers here and to look for ways of removing dissolved chemicals.

The competitive trends in the market are far from clear. Some of A. Bailey's foreign competitors have already run into trouble from underestimating the difficulties and costs involved in working so far from home. The future of some of the foreign companies seems to depend more on status and politics than on sound economic factors. The Australian market is small and fragmented, and the competitors have resorted to maintaining a minimum staff of salespeople to run the offices.

Another unknown in this industry is the future influence of consulting engineers. Most municipalities are too small to be able to afford their own experts in sewage plant selection and construction. This function is carried out mainly by consultants. A. Bailey can also put its expert staff at the service of a municipality.

The formation of a government body to help the municipalities design their plants cannot be ignored. There is a marked tendency to reduce the reliance upon direct labor in the operation of treatment plants. The controls are now being brought to one central control room overlooking the plant. Before long, one can expect to see completely automated plants.

For Australia and many other countries, water supply and sewage treatment are inextricably linked. Water is converted into effluent in every home, factory, and office. Fresh water is getting scarcer while consumption is going up. The time will come when most sewage will have to be converted to fresh water, which would seem to solve the problem.

It will not, however, since there are inevitable losses from evaporation, seepage, and poisoning. Planners are worried that within generations, water demands may be such that supplies of fresh water will be insufficient to make up for losses.

Large municipalities have their own sewage experts. Their new treatment plants are worth millions of dollars each, and the international companies compete fiercely to win their contracts, in spite of the fact that the large municipalities are fussy clients. Small municipalities normally employ consultants to carry out feasibility studies, recommend processes, and run the contracts.

Jeff also learned that the Ministry of Water Affairs Effluent Research Unit was taking an active interest and that some interesting processes were under development in their laboratories.

The Current Position for A. Bailey (Pty), Ltd.

Jeff Bailey's problem is to expand his company's share of the market and to make certain that his operations are profitable. Although A. Bailey (Pty), Ltd., is a local company, it still imports 75 percent of its equipment from the United Kingdom, Germany, and the United States, which is then modified for local conditions.

Jeff Bailey has to decide what to do. He will undertake a political strategy!

To cover a lot of detailed ground as painlessly as possible, let us summarize the main conclusions that emerged from the economic strategy analysis that Bailey made (along the lines of Hofer and Schendel 1978) and then proceed to the political strategy phase.

Analysis of the Total Situation

The material parts of the system are summarized in Figure 9.1. Bailey gets equipment from overseas suppliers (1) and modifies it. Competitors' sales offices get equipment from overseas principals (2). Bailey and the competitors supply their equipment to two major markets: sewage plants to municipalities (3) and effluent plants to industry (4). At present, about 70 percent of the sewage equipment market is in large towns and cities. The two markets are regulated by legislation (5) that is administered by the Ministry of Water Affairs (6), which also supports the Effluent Research Unit (7). Both municipalities (8) and industry (9) are served by consultants, who advise on the installation of new plants.

Figure 9.1   Analysis of the Total Situation

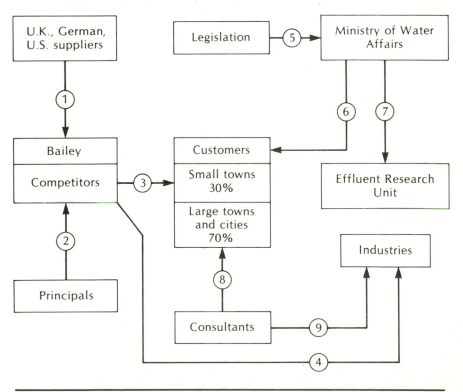

After some consideration of the trends in the environment, Jeff Bailey decided that the following were the major threat and opportunity.

Major Threat.   Bailey would not be able to keep current with new technology being developed by the huge overseas principals of the competitors and would be bypassed.

Major Opportunity.   Bailey could establish itself as a local service-oriented effluent treatment and water recovery equipment supplier. Other alternatives, such as becoming a consultant or selling out, were considered but rejected for various reasons. (Being a consultant conflicts with being an equipment supplier, which is where the company's major investment is now. In addition, there is currently an "oversupply" of consultants.) The political strategy should therefore be focused on creating conditions in the environment that will enhance the opportunity of developing as a local service-oriented company in the face of major competitors who can bypass the company via new technology.

POLITICAL ANALYSIS: OPPORTUNITY FOR BAILEY

To start formulating the political strategy, we must first analyze the total situation from a political perspective. As was mentioned in Chapter 7, each of the cases will be used to highlight different aspects of the whole process of political strategy. In this case, the focus is on unfolding and identifying the implications of the situation to key decision makers in each critical area.

The first analysis is concerned with the decision-making process for sewage equipment supply in a municipality or an industrial plant. There appear to be two major types of systems in municipalities.

For Large Municipalities

For large municipalities, the process is depicted in Figure 9.2.

The townspeople via a voting process (1) elect a town council (2), which appoints a town engineer (3), who in turn appoints sewage experts (4) and other departments to run sewage plants (6) that provide sewage treatment and other services to the town (7). In the selection of equipment, the sewage experts and the town engineers tend to use consultants (8) or to consult other town engineers (9) to develop a specification for the plant, and then a public call for quotes is made via the town council (10), which, under advisement

Figure 9.2   Equipment Selection Decisions in Municipalities

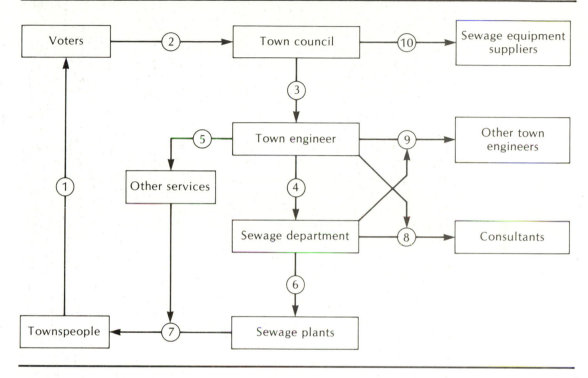

from the town engineer, selects from the contracts submitted by the equipment suppliers.

For Small Municipalities

The main difference for small municipalities is that the town engineer does not have the funds for a sewage department expert and generally has to act as "expert" for all the services such as gas, electricity, water, sewage, and roads. He is therefore in a much more difficult position as far as equipment selection and operation is concerned. He must rely far more heavily on inputs from other town engineers or, if he can afford it, consultants.

For Industrial Plants

Essentially, a similar equipment selection process occurs in industrial plants. It is, however, usually the works engineer who develops the specifications and the board or capital committee that puts out the contract. Once again, large industries tend to have effluent experts in-house, while small industries tend to regard the works manager as the "resident effluent expert."

Bailey must recognize that there are several key factors in these decision-making systems. First, it is the town engineer or works engineer who is held responsible for plant operation and who thus has a major vested interest in the equipment selection decisions.

Second, sewage and effluent plants are not exactly in the mainstream of the community or industry activity, but they are a considerable nuisance when they are not functioning correctly. Both effluent and sewage plants are most visible to the constituents when they are not working. The engineer is rarely commended for how well they are working and is generally the focus of a lot of negative inputs when they are not.

Third, the smaller the organization, the more serious it is for the engineer, since he cannot draw on in-house expertise to get the plant in operation again.

What begins to emerge here is that the engineer, particularly of small operations, will be concerned with two factors that will be of critical interest to him in selection of equipment: reliability, in that he does not want it to break down, and service when it does.

POLITICAL STRATEGY
FORMULATION: OPPORTUNITY FOR BAILEY

Let us now go back and look at Bailey's situation in a power and influence context. What Bailey can do at this point that none of its competitors can do is to provide specific after-sales service. It is the only player in the equipment supplier industry that has the people qualified to get a malfunctioning plant back to normal under local conditions. This strength constitutes a particular inducement to the potential purchasers and is thus a power resource. The question is whether it is strategic.

To decide, we must look at the competitors' position. At present, they are trying to keep overheads down in a highly fragmented and not particularly rich market. They are operating sales offices and do not have the field personnel to provide breakdown service in a big way. Even if they wanted to do so, they need time and resources to train people to operate the equipment under local conditions.

The fact is that Bailey's inducement resource (service) therefore constitutes an important strategic power resource, because the engineers have limited alternatives and the competitors will need time to replicate this service—if they can afford to do so at all!

However, Bailey has the problem of convincing the engineers that the service is worthwhile and that it will be available. The traditional approach might be to undertake an intensive industrial marketing effort. The political approach calls for a detailed political analysis with the intent of restructuring conditions so that Bailey can achieve the same purposes.

If we think about it, the basic problem is one of persuading the targets—a problem of changing perceptions. We therefore need to consider influence processes.

Let us analyze the system developed in Figure 9.2 and ask ourselves where the dominant influence patterns are. To have influence, we need to establish audience, provide strategic information, and control commitments. The question we should ask ourselves is who in the system has audience with the town engineer (or works engineer in the industrial effluent case). The key influencers in the process of equipment selection appear to be other town engineers (via the grapevine) and particularly the consultants. If Jeff Bailey can induce the consultants to recommend him rather than others, he will be in a strong position.

A consultant is ill-advised to ally herself to a particular manufacturer, for fear of besmirching her reputation for objectivity (one of the reasons Bailey did not think it could operate a credible consulting service and still be an equipment supplier). However, we need to explore the dependency relation between consultant and engineer in more detail.

The role of the consultant is to assist the engineer in writing a specification that will go out to public contract. What Bailey would want to have is a situation in which the alternatives available to the town council are reduced to one: A. Bailey, Ltd. He has something to offer that no other manufacturer can offer, and that is field service. Therefore, if he can get the specifications written in such a way that after-sales service is guaranteed as a condition of contract, he will effectively lock out his competitors, who cannot meet this guarantee.

The problem, then, becomes one of inducing the consultants to include this guarantee. How do we do this? We return to the analysis of the dependency relation between consultant and engineer.

Let us now look at the process whereby the engineer chooses a consultant. The chances are that either he will use one he has used successfully before, or he will go through the grapevine and ask other engineers what they think. The consultants are in competition with one another, and they compete on the basis of reputation via the grapevine. Consulting engineers generally do not advertise, so it is difficult to break into the grapevine and more difficult to differentiate themselves from equally competent consultants. If a consultant can find a way of differentating herself from her competitors in a way that enhances her reputation, she will welcome it.

Once Bailey recognizes this, it is easy to see that a consultant has a high incentive to write a specification that contains a clause requiring certain after-sales breakdown service guarantees. In this way, she becomes the only consultant in the industry that demands this highly beneficial clause.

For those engineers who consider such protection important, the consultant's prestige will be considerably enhanced. For those engineers with in-house expertise, the clause may not be all that important, but the fact that it was available would still make the consultant's role as a protector of their interests dramatically visible.

If Bailey can get one consultant to include this clause in one contract, the grapevine will start transmitting it. Instead of a vague promise of service, a tangible guarantee is offered.

But what will happen now? Other consultants may be forced to "match the offer." If they do this, where does that leave the initiating consultant?

Here lies the key for Bailey's negotiation with that first consultant. If other consultants are eventually going to follow suit, then the only differentiation that the first consultant can achieve is being the first one in the industry to introduce the clause. And the more "successful" the clause is, the more important it is to be the first. Therefore, in the negotiation with the consultant he selects, Bailey has a powerful bargaining base. In effect, he is giving the consultant an opportunity that can easily be given to someone else.

It therefore appears that the environment can be restructured to suit Bailey's purpose by an influence play, after which he will emerge as the only alternative available to those engineers who want guaranteed after-sales breakdown service.

The tentative alliance that he needs to create as far as his opportunity is concerned is with a number of consultants whose only contribution will be to include a breakdown service guarantee in the contract specification. His first move should be to find just one consultant who is prepared to do this.

STRATEGIC ANTICIPATION: OPPORTUNITY FOR BAILEY

How will the competitors respond? First, we have seen that competitors have succeeded in taking away many engineers by taking them to "inspect" overseas plants. Bailey has not matched this move, and the chances are that competitors will increase these types of efforts in response to the guarantee clause.

Second, we can expect them to start moving toward a more service-oriented business. Perhaps some will consider importing and training a field force. They will probably consider luring away Bailey's own people to join them and provide this service.

Let us now look at the problem of establishing service-oriented businesses from the perspective of the decision makers in the competitors' organizations. It appears that they are under pressure to keep overheads down. Any additions to personnel, particularly ones in which there is a long lag between incurring the expense and getting benefits from the expense, will make their position here difficult with the overseas headquarters. It is therefore more likely that if they match Bailey at all, they will try to do it by drawing away Bailey's personnel. Bailey must ensure that his field experts are given little incentive to move.

Also, Bailey's competitors appear to be more interested in the large plants. Small, remote plants are probably regarded as a necessary evil. It seems likely that they will gladly forgo that part of the market initially.

Finally, this is a situation of many customers and few competitors. It is going to be expensive for each competitor in the industry as a whole to develop and maintain a field sales force.

The interesting possibility that emerges from the analysis is that Bailey can undertake breakdown service (and commissioning, perhaps) on behalf of the entire industry by structuring a subsidiary that will subcontract breakdown work for all installations that desire it.

Once Bailey has recovered sufficient share of the market to have the impact of his strategy sufficiently severe that the competitors will start considering a countermove, he can stabilize that share by approaching them with the rational offer of creating a (lucrative for him) field breakdown service subsidiary. The theme of his negtioting strategy here will be that he will be saving each member of the industry the cost of taking on, training, and maintaining their own field service teams. Remember that they are currently under pressure to keep costs down in the highly fragmented and rather unprofitable market they face. In exchange for doing so, he may convince them to stay out of the small plant market entirely and leave it to him.

Let us return now to the other response he can expect, that of increased overseas trips for potential buyers. What Bailey needs to recognize is that he too has overseas principals whose large equipment he imports and who would like to see him regain his share of the market. If he elects to match his competitors' rather dubious sales methods, there is no reason that the principals should not share in the costs of such methods. The theme emerges again: Why try to do something on our own if we can find allies who are able to assist us?

POLITICAL STRATEGY: OPPORTUNITY FOR BAILEY

With regard to the opportunity for Bailey, we see the following offensive and defensive strategies emerging.

Offensive Strategy

Exploit Targets' Weaknesses.   Form an alliance with one or more consultants to have a guaranteed breakdown service clause included in the contract specification. Such an alliance should firmly secure a large part of the small-plant market and some of the large-plant market.

Erode Targets' Strengths.   Match targets' overseas junket offer with offers supported in large part by Bailey's overseas suppliers, provided this inducement is not against Bailey's principles.

Defensive Strategy

Block Erosion of Bailey's Own Strengths.   When competitors start showing signs of matching Bailey with their own field force (someone in A. Bailey, Ltd., will be approached to join such a force), propose that Bailey form a subsidiary that will provide industry-wide breakdown maintenance.

Prevent Exploitation of Bailey's Own Weaknesses.   In this case, the strategy is the same as eroding targets' strengths.

POLITICAL ANALYSIS: MAJOR THREAT TO BAILEY

The major threat Bailey sees is that due to the lack of resources, the company cannot invest the funds to keep abreast of technology. He runs the risk of being "leapfrogged" and left behind. The political approach argues that if he does not have the resources to do something, he should try to find someone who will do it for him. In Bailey's case, the organizations to do it for him are obvious: his overseas suppliers and the Effluent Research Unit of the Ministry of Water Affairs.

Starting with the Effluent Research Unit, we are going to focus in this case on the decision-making systems of our targets. Let us look at the system in some detail.

Bailey must ask himself what type of person works in such a department, where the pay is often less than elsewhere in the country. There appear to be three types: (1) people who, out of a sense of dedication to the patriotic need for Australia to handle its water problems, want to help; (2) people who, out of dedication to science, want to do research; and (3) people who enjoy the security of a government job.

If the key decision makers in the Effluent Research Unit are of the first or second type, then Bailey has a high chance of establishing audience with them, because he is a "lone Australian doing battle with large overseas interests"—which could appeal to the patriots. He is also the acknowledged Australian expert and has a wealth of practical knowledge regarding the design, development, and operation of sewage and effluent plants under Australian conditions—which could appeal to the scientists.

Ideally, Bailey should establish an alliance with members of the Effluent Research Unit whereby he can keep up-to-date in technology. He needs to consider what he can bring to such an alliance, such as:

1. If he takes the trouble to secure it, information from his German, British, and American principals on the state of the art in the technology of these countries and materials on the latest developments in their research efforts.

2. Equipment, field personnel, and occasionally funds that will be useful for the researchers in supplementing the funds they need to carry out research projects.

3. Knowledge regarding the applications and operation of actual plants, knowledge of plant conditions and operational changes required under different conditions in Australia.

4. Actual plants out in the field on which pilot research or full-scale research can be carried out, together with a field force who can get it working again when things go wrong!

From the points of view of the Effluent Research Unit scientists, there are substantial benefits in working with Bailey in bringing new technology to fruition under Australian conditions. They can work on the basic research, and he can help them convert from basic research to applications.

STRATEGIC ANTICIPATION: THREAT TO BAILEY

How would the competitors respond to a move by Bailey to start working with the Effluent Research Unit?

The question is whether they will do anything at all! At present, they cannot match what Bailey can bring to the unit, and at this point they are under severe profit pressure, so there are not many funds. They are unlikely to be able to understand the results of the research or to carry out the conversions. And, finally, they are not Australian.

As time goes by, these conditions are likely to change. More sophisticated operations are likely to be set up by the competitors as the market expands to justify them. If Bailey is to take advantage of his position, it must be in the few years before these more sophisticated operations are installed. If any of the competitors does try to move closer, Bailey can, by performance, take every opportunity to demonstrate time and again the vast difference between what he can bring to the Effluent Research Unit and what they can bring.

Over the next few years, an intensely reciprocative and personal relationship between Bailey and the Effluent Research Unit can be developed. Then, when the competitors try to move in, Bailey will have developed a great deal of audience with the unit, and it will take a long time for it to erode.

POLITICAL STRATEGY: MAJOR THREAT TO BAILEY

Offensive Strategy

Exploit Targets' Weaknesses.   Use the fact that Bailey is Australian and experienced in Australian operations to secure audience. Emphasize that at this stage, the competition cannot meet these requirements.

Erode Targets' Strengths.   Develop a position of audience with the Effluent Research Unit and a working relationship whereby Bailey and the unit undertake joint projects in converting new Australian technology to operating plants.

Defensive Strategy

Prevent Erosion of Bailey's Strengths.   Demonstrate, via performance, the vast difference between Bailey and competitors in capability to convert from laboratory to full-scale operation.

Prevent Exploitation of Bailey's Weaknesses.   Input latest technology via Bailey's overseas suppliers to the Effluent Research Unit.

CONCLUSION

This concludes the political strategy for this case. Once again, it must be emphasized that the cases are illustrative rather than comprehensive. For this reason, the discussion was restricted to one opportunity and one threat. In a real-life situation, more opportunities and threats would be identified and explored by similar processes. Options unexplored, for instance, include the possibility of merging with a larger competitor. (In such an event, however, Bailey should go to the merger from a position of strength, with regained market share and a robust competitive position.)

In this case, the prime focus was on looking at the nature of the decision-making that takes place in the stakeholders' systems. We saw that through exploration of the dependencies between these stakeholders and their systems, the possibilities for indirect political action became evident. (In the previous case, Alpha Oil Mills, more attention was given to relations between systems, and we focused on the process of carrying out a political strategy formulation.)

In the next case, more attention is given to analysis of alternative structures and formulation of negotiating strategies.

10

Illustrative Case Study: Apollo Wholesalers

APOLLO WHOLESALER'S PROBLEM

Jack Walliser, managing director of Apollo Wholesalers, a household products wholesaler, was faced with a problem in the sales of a bar soap. (Bar soap is a crude, low-quality form of soap produced in large bars. It is used in more remote areas for home laundering.)

Bar soap is extremely sensitive to transport costs and can therefore be produced only locally. Walliser is certain that he is facing a pricing arrangement between the five local producers, whose share of the local market is shown in Table 10.1.

Aleph is an international company that markets a large number of products, whereas Vau is a small regional company that produces only bar soap. Apollo Wholesalers is one of four major local wholesaling companies (Table 10.2) that supply a number of retail outlets in the region.

The balance of bar soap sales is made directly from producer to three major retail chains, whose market shares are shown in Table 10.3.

No retailer other than the chain stores has more than 1 percent of the market. Bar soap is unbranded. It is basically packed into wooden boxes after being wrapped in plastic and then is sold direct from these boxes to the public. Walliser is wondering what he should do about the suspected cartel that appears to have a price agreement going. What has been happening is that all wholesalers buy bar soap from all the producers. Walliser has been trying every means at his disposal to get a price reduction from the producers, but no matter which supplier he approaches, he gets the same price. The other wholesalers appear to be getting the same treatment.

Table 10.1   Five Local Producers of Bar Soap and Their Market Shares

Producer	Competitive Status	Bar Soap's Status in Company's Product Line	Approximate Retail Market Share of Bar Soap Sales
Aleph	International	One of many product lines	40%
Beth	International	One of many product lines	30%
Gimel	National	One of limited product lines	15%
Daleth	Local	Sole (marginal) product	10%
Vau	Local	Sole (marginal) product	5%

Walliser knows that in recent years, the market for bar soap has been eroded by the introduction of a more sophisticated product (bulk detergent), and this has caused some overcapacity in the industry. He would therefore expect the two local producers, who are battling for profits, to be interested in coming to some kind of price reduction agreement just to increase volume.

The reasons Walliser wants to effect a reduction in the price of bar soap are threefold:

1. Retailers are complaining that the chain stores are selling bar soap at prices that can only mean that the chain stores are getting a big price break from the producers. Consequently, they are asking for a price break for themselves.
2. Walliser has noticed with some concern the steady growth chain stores are achieving in the retail market. The retailers are starting to talk about forming buyers' cooperatives to develop more clout by buying in large quantities directly from the producers.

Table 10.2   Four Local Wholesalers and Their Market Shares

Wholesaler	Approximate Retail Market Share for Bar Soap
Apollo	25%
Castor	20%
Pollux	10%
Achilles	10%

Table 10.3   Three Retail Chains and Their Market Shares

Chain Stores	Approximate Retail Market Share for Bar Soap
Wodan	15%
Thor	15%
Freia	5%

Walliser feels that the days of the wholesaler dominating the household products market are numbered but also recognizes that once the shakeout is over, there will always be a role to be played by the surviving wholesalers. Walliser is determined to be one of the surviving wholesalers.

3. Though 5 percent of sales may sound low, for a wholesaler this is a significant percentage of total sales. In effect, this was the second largest revenue generator in his business.

To resolve his concerns, Walliser has to take market share away from the competitors. He must demonstrate to the retailers that he has the ability to deliver superior performance, and bar soap appears that it might be a useful test case.

The decision he must make is whether to go up against the cartel of suppliers and, if so, how to go about it.

ANALYSIS OF THE TOTAL SITUATION

The total situation is analyzed in Figure 10.1.

The system here depicts the flow of bar soap from production to retailer. In addition to bar soap, the wholesaler handles a large number of other lines of household products. Many of these are supplied to Apollo through Aleph, Beth, and Gimel, who have mul-

Figure 10.1 Analysis of the Bar Soap System

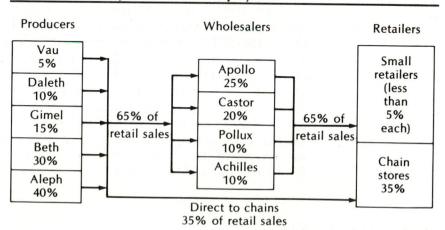

Note: Figures in blocks represent total retail market sales of bar soap.

Figure 10.2   Apollo Wholesalers' Overall Sales Structure

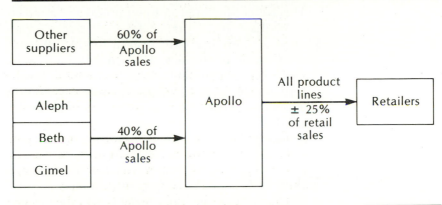

tiple lines of products, including the competing product bulk detergent, which now constitutes a good 5 percent of sales but appears to be leveling off.

Walliser must take care not to antagonize the producers, who currently supply him with about 40 percent of his total sales. Suppliers of other products account for the remaining 60 percent of his total sales.

Finally, for each of the product lines that Apollo handles, Walliser's sales are in the region of 25 percent of the retail market, as with bar soap.

The prior discussion is summarized in Figure 10.2.

The critical elements in the system are obviously the chain stores and producers, who are potential targets in a price cut play, and other wholesalers and retailers who would benefit from a price cut and who are thus potential allies. However, since Walliser is intent on cutting into the other wholesalers' market share, this disqualifies them as allies. He also feels that the small retailers are individually too weak and collectively too dispersed and disorganized to be of much use. The attempt at political strategy should therefore be viewed as something he will have to do on his own. The first step is an analysis of the targets, in which Walliser attempts to determine the system flows of his targets.

ANALYSIS OF TARGETS

Analysis of the targets reveals that there are three major types of targets.

International Producers

The system for international producers appears in Figure 10.3.

Walliser finds that the international producers are producing most of their bar soap from a waste product (called fatty acid) of their other operations. Low-quality fatty acid is converted to bar soap. For both international producers, however, insufficient fatty acid waste is available, so low-quality tallow is purchased from outside suppliers, and about 20 percent of final sales is purchased for this purpose. Walliser also finds that bar soap is about 2 percent or less of each company's total sales.

National Producer (Gimel)

The system for the national producer is similar. Gimel also produces bar soap from low-quality waste fatty acid, but in its case about 15 percent of total sales are made from poor-quality tallows purchased from outside suppliers. Bar soap sales are also about 2 percent of Gimel's total sales.

Regional Producers

Daleth and Vau, whose sole product is bar soap, produce all their sales from tallow purchased from outside suppliers.

Finally, Walliser is aware that the pattern of replacement of bar

Figure 10.3   International Producers: Bar Soap System

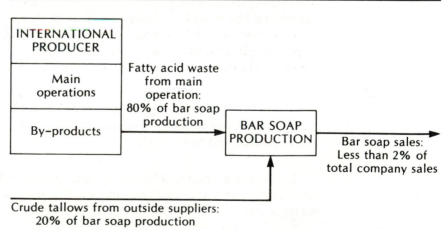

soap by the bulk detergent is not too dissimilar from his own experience with the sales of these products. Over the years, his proportion of sales of bar soap has fallen from about 8 percent to the current level of about 5 percent.

What does the information really mean?

Walliser knows that there is overcapacity in the industry. If sales have fallen from 8 to 5 percent, he can estimate that industrywide capacity must be in the region of five-eighths, or about 60 percent of the capacity they used to supply.

He also knows that sitting with excess capacity is expensive and that there is a high incentive to reduce overhead cost per unit sales by increasing volume. This type of reduction is usually achieved by cutting prices, but if there is overcapacity in the industry, price wars result, which can be avoided by a price cartel (which he appears to be facing).

However, if there is overcapacity in the industry, he knows that a great incentive exists for someone to cheat. In particular, if people can find a way of cheating without being punished, they will have even more incentive to cheat.

In looking at his array of targets, Walliser has to decide who would have the highest incentive to cheat. The obvious ones are Daleth and Vau, the two regional purchasers whose sole product is bar soap and who are at present running marginal operations.

Now Walliser can do some calculating.

Currently, Apollo is selling 25 percent of the market. Combined, Daleth and Vau are supplying 15 percent of the market. If they had held market share as the market declined, they should have capacity to supply $8/5 \times 15$, or about 24 percent of the market. The main thing that would stop them from cutting prices to gain market share would be the punitive retaliation from the other, larger producers.

However, let us look now at the decison-making systems of the other producers. Bar soap sales constitute a small proportion of their total sales, which raises some interesting questions:

1. What is the reason for a cartel in the first place?
2. What kind of decision maker is going to be making the decisions regarding bar soap prices?

If we take a good look at the system shown in Figure 10.3, we can perhaps see the answer to question 1. Bar soap is a profitable way of getting rid of what would otherwise be a major nuisance: fatty acid waste. The last thing that any of the big producers would want to get stuck with is a waste product piling up at the end of their production systems. The only reason they would want to come to some kind of stabilizing cartel arrangement would be to stop the smaller producers from taking away market share, thus causing the big producers to have fatty acid piling up in their warehouses. Once a stabilized situation has been reached, at a profitable price, why not buy some low-quality fatty acid and turn more of a profit making more bar soap?

But the purpose of risking a cartel agreement is to stop waste fatty acid from piling up, not to hold prices. If such is the case, more figuring can be done. At present, about 20 percent of Aleph's and Beth's sales and 10 percent of Gimel's sales of bar soap are made from outside supplies. With Aleph and Beth having 70 percent of the current market and Gimel having 15 percent, this means that $(0.20 \times 70) + (0.1 \times 15)$, or about 15 percent of their current sales are made from outside supplies.

Let's put the figuring all together. Apollo sells 25 percent of the retail market. Daleth and Vau sell 15 percent together but could possibly produce another 8 percent, making about 23 percent of the retail market. And Aleph, Beth, and Gimel can lose a total of 15 percent of the market before they start getting violent about price cuts.

It appears that it may be possible to persuade Daleth and Vau to join in an alliance with Apollo to cut their prices in exchange for a guaranteed increase in volume to about 60 percent more than they are currently producing, yet still not reach a market share level that will get the opposition to a point where they are not able to use up their current waste. The question is, how likely are the big producers to accept this arrangement without taking punitive action?

STRATEGIC ANTICIPATION

How will the big producers respond? To answer this, we need the answer to question 2 asked before: What kind of decision maker is going to make the bar soap price decision?

The question Walliser had to ask himself was, "If I were in charge of a large international company operating in this country, whom would I put in charge of a waste product operation that sells less than 2 percent of my total sales?" The answer would not be a hard-minded, aggressive, and sharp manager destined for the top. Walliser could guess that the person in charge of bar soap activities would almost certainly be someone who would not be prepared to rock the boat. He would be more concerned with not piling up waste in front of production processes making main-line products, because he would be assessed more on disruption of production than on departmental profits.

What it boils down to is that if Walliser gets into the decision-making level of the target, he recognizes that he is not taking on the mighty Aleph or Beth or Gimel as organizations but is taking on a person—in this case a person who probably has little political capability. The main thing he must do is keep from causing that person to panic. He needs to be persuaded that he is not going to face a problem of excess fatty acids.

If Walliser plays his cards right and negotiates well, he can anticipate that Aleph, Beth, and Gimel will hold prices and reduce production by reducing outside purchases. The next step is to develop a negotiating strategy.

NEGOTIATING STRATEGY

For all the targets, the main issue appears to be one of *price* at this stage. What Walliser must do is break the coalitions by focusing attention on the *volume* issue. He knew that he had sufficient sales to be able to handle all the volume, up to Vau and Daleth's original capacity, if they decided to give him a price break. He also wanted to lock his competitors out of any price reduction if possible, because he was intent on a grander strategy of demonstrating to retailers that Apollo was the wholesaler they should support. This introduced a third issue: *exclusivity* of price reductions. Walliser accordingly set down the issues and their priorities for each party (Table 10.4).

When we consider the issues in terms of priorities, we see three distinct patterns emerge. If Walliser cannot get some exclusivity, he may as well not get price reductions, so exclusivity is his first priority. He knows he can handle the volume, so volume is his lowest priority.

For the small producers, the issue of volume is probably the most urgent. If they can raise their volumes, they can increase profits and to some extent can reduce prices. The least of their worries is Walliser's concern with exclusivity.

Table 10.4 Issue Priorities in Negotiation

Issue	Walliser	Small Producers	Big Producers
Price	2	2	1
Volume	3	1	2 conditional
Exclusivity	1	3	3

For the big producers, the issue of price is paramount, because they can adjust volume via outside purchases. However, if volume falls below a certain level, price becomes unimportant. They too could care less about Walliser's concern with exclusivity.

It is obvious from looking at these issues that two separate negotiating strategies are required: one for small and one for big producers.

Walliser should negotiate first with the small producers to ascertain their interest in increasing volume and then with the large producers to allay their fears that they will end up in a position of oversupply. He can allay their fears only when he has some assurance that he will have the support of the smaller producers.

In formulating his negotiation strategy for the smaller producers, the order for negotiating appears to be volume, price, and exclusivity for the following reasons. Walliser can start the negotiations by implying that he is considering increasing his orders to take up to 150 percent of their current total orders, and he wants to know whether this is possible.

Once the small producers have become thoroughly interested in this, Walliser can start talking price. The key bluff Walliser can use is that if he does not get what he wants from the small producer, he can go to the others. He will then reveal that he has sufficient evidence of a price agreement to make things rather uncomfortable if the suppliers act uncooperatively. He will also reveal that he is prepared to arrange with the other producers for them not to take punitive action.

When the small producers still show reluctance to take a price cut, Walliser can suggest that he take an option to buy all their production for the next two years, provided it does not exceed 150 percent of their current total sales. The option will have a time limit, and if Walliser exercises the option, he will agree to a contract in which a price, to be agreed later, is set. In this way, he can guarantee his exclusivity without even having it enter the agenda as a bargaining point. (Notice the difference if he starts the negotiation with the issue of exclusivity; it would provide the producer with a lever.)

Once Walliser has the options, he can go to the large producers, where the agenda would be price, volume, and exclusivity, in that order.

Here, Walliser can start negotiations by emphasizing that he has no intention of changing the price structure of the large producers, but that he intends taking far more volume from the small producers, which will probably reduce the large producers' market share. He will hasten to add that this will in no way reduce their volume to the extent that they will be sitting with excess stock. Apollo will be prepared to take off any excess stock at current prices, if they want Apollo to do so. To demonstrate his commitment, Walliser will show them the options he has taken out with the small producers, thus also avoiding the threat they could make to the small producers (since they are committed to the transgressive act via their options). Faced with this situation, the large producers have no incentive to cut prices. Walliser obviously would prefer that they did not; hence his offer to continue to buy from them a reduced volume at their existing prices. Once again, if Walliser succeeds, he has maintained exclusivity without the issue entering the agenda.

With this strategy in mind, Walliser can now approach the small producers with the intention of negotiating a reduced price. (Or can he? The political approach suggests that having identified critical allies or targets, he may find it worthwhile to investigate their dependencies to probe for possible areas of indirect action. This part of the analysis has not been done.)

STRATEGY IMPLEMENTATION

In the actual case, Walliser took his negotiating strategy to the small producers and found two bitter people. A formerly lucrative business had slowly been eroded away by declining markets for bar soap; they were both sitting with about 55 percent of their capacity unused but were still carrying the overhead costs of the equipment and maintenance. They were desperate to increase volume but felt that any price cut would launch a major price war that they could not survive.

Both expressed great interest in Walliser's proposal, but then the bombshell exploded. They were strapped not only on the output side but also on the input side. Walliser had failed to explore *their* dependencies, and both producers depended on outside suppliers for fatty acid to make their product.

The fatty acid system is depicted in Figure 10.4.

Walliser found that Daleth and Vau depended for their supplies of fatty acid on three major suppliers, Alpha, Beta, and Gamma, who produced low-quality crude tallow as a by-product from the production of canned meats. Moreover, Alpha, Beta, and Gamma together purchased more than half of the production of this crude tallow, and the suppliers were in a difficult position: They had to sell it or also have their production systems held up by excess inventories of waste product.

By acting in concert, Aleph, Beth, and Gimel had been able to take control of the raw material supply system. They were, to some extent, independent of the suppliers because they produced most of their raw material in-house. By selectively "punishing" recalcitrant suppliers (merely canceling orders and letting the waste inventory

Figure 10.4   System for Fatty Acid:
Sales of Waste Fatty Acid Bought by Producers

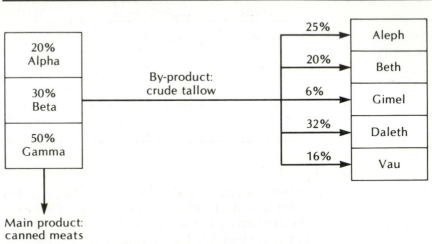

pile up), they were eventually able to control how much tallow would be sold to each producer and thus controlled the tallow market. Even if Daleth or Vau wanted to increase volume, they might not get the raw materials for it!

As it happened, canned meat was one of Apollo's lines (25 percent of total retail sales). With this additional information, a new dimension is added. Walliser can break the control of Aleph, Beth, and Gimel by guaranteeing to Alpha, Beta, and Gamma that he will buy up all their production of crude tallow.

Alpha, Beta, and Gamma currently supply tallow as shown in Table 10.5.

Moreover, Apollo has a lot of clout with Alpha, Beta, and Gamma because Apollo is currently buying 25 percent of their output. Walliser must recognize that here is an opportunity for Apollo to get total control of the situation by taking an option to buy all of Alpha, Beta, and Gamma's tallow production. He can thus guarantee the *suppliers* that their waste tallow will be purchased, can guarantee *Daleth* and *Vau* that they will have sufficient supplies of tallow to produce all the bar soap they want, and can guarantee to buy it from them (at his prices). He can then control the amount of outside tallow that *Aleph*, *Beth*, and *Gimel* can get to make extra product. And he has the sales capacity to sell at least 25 percent of the market.

With the option to buy all the outside tallow, Walliser has provided Aleph, Beth, and Gimel's managers a plausible reason to give their bosses for the decrease in sales volume: There is a shortage of

Table 10.5   Percentage of Tallow Supplied by Alpha, Beta, and Gamma

Company Supplied	Percentage of Tallow Bought Outside	Total Bar Soap Sales
Aleph	20% of 40%	8
Beth	20% of 30%	6
Gimel	15% of 15%	2
Daleth	100% of 10%	10
Vau	100% of 5%	5
Total		±31% of the total bar soap retail sales

outside tallow to make the product! Finally, there is no incentive for them to reduce prices to Apollo's competitors, so Apollo can obtain the exclusivity it is seeking if it can ensure that the large producers do not cut prices. Walliser's negotiating strategy is now enhanced by the fact that he can ally himself with the suppliers first, to secure an option to buy all their output, then go to the small producers with an offer they can't refuse and secure options for their production, and then go to the large producers with all these options and get them to recognize that he holds the cards but will not threaten their waste disposal problem.

(As a matter of record, Walliser managed to effect a substantial price decrease and increased Apollo's market share in bar soap to 30 percent within a year. Five years later, by applying political strategies to its other lines, Apollo ended up with 60 percent of the regional wholesale market.)

SUMMARY

In an actual political strategy situation, it is rarely necessary to apply in detail all the concepts discussed in this book, but at different times and in different situations, each of the concepts has proved useful in the formulation of a political strategy. The procedure outlined in Chapter 7, then, need not be copied slavishly but rather should be used as a guideline for checking whether all the facets that should be considered have been considered.

In this case, we focused on two aspects of strategy that received less emphasis in the other cases: detailed analyses of the dependency structures and alternative structures of the players, and negotiating strategy, a simple three-issue, two-step negotiating process in this case.

11

Illustrative Case Study: Herbicide Division of Mid-West Chemical Company

THE PROBLEM

Dr. Bill Plummer had recently been assigned the job of building up the herbicide business of Mid-West Chemical, a major U.S. chemical manufacturer. Plummer knew he had a problem when the results of the most recent survey of dealers' and distributors' attitudes to Mid-West Chemical Company came in. Mid-West had been ranked seventh out of seven by those in the sample. Some had been so angry as to write in additional numbers to try to rank his company tenth out of seven.

Several years before, Mid-West Chemical had embarked on an ill-fated move into the higher-margin specialty chemicals in an attempt to reduce the company's major problem, namely poor profits from their commodity chemical business. Instead of solving their problems, the move had doubled them; the company could not gear up to developing, manufacturing, and marketing specialty chemicals.

THE SITUATION

Mid-West's recent mismanagement of the marketing of their herbicide called Deadem was a case in point. Mid-West Chemical had launched a huge and surprisingly effective campaign to sell the Midwest corn and soybean farmers on this product. The campaign had used a combined strategy: a push strategy of loading up the distributors' shelves through special promotions was reinforced by an attempt to sell some dealers directly, bypassing the distributors. In addition, Mid-West established retail outlets that sold directly to the farmer. The sales force and advertising copy virtually promised to kill every weed in the United States—and, surprisingly, the traditionally conservative farming community had believed the campaign and bought Deadem in vast quantities. However, after multiple applications, it became clear to most farmers that Deadem not only did *not* kill many weeds unless weather conditions were very humid but also *did* cause delayed, but nonetheless painful, irritation of the skin after multiple exposure; hence, the ranking of Mid-West Chemical's credibility. Words like "snake oil sellers" were not uncommon in farming communities whenever Mid-West was mentioned, perhaps explaining the recent vacancy in the senior management position in Mid-West's herbicide business—the one that Plummer had just filled.

Plummer knew that his problem was one that was not likely to go away quickly or without sustained effort. Farmers have long memories and forgive slowly. They lead lonely and difficult lives, fighting weather, pestilence, and highly competitive markets. They feel that this hardship should not be complicated further by false promises from fast-talking city folk. Their recent experience with Deadem did much to reinforce their feeling that "only a damn fool rushes out and tries every newfangled gimmick or product that comes on the market." Not surprisingly, their reception of the Mid-West Chemical sales force was less than cordial. The fact that the sales force was also greeted with enraged abuse by disappointed distributors did little for their morale.

Plummer did have some good news, though. The test results of their new herbicide, Rodeo, were exceptionally promising, particularly for broad-leaved crops in the Midwest. The problem was how to get Rodeo accepted in the marketplace in the wake of the Deadem fiasco—a classic problem in developing an influence strategy.

The herbicide business can be viewed as consisting of several overlapping market segments. The first segmentation is by type of crop. Corn is a narrow-leaved crop (like a large grass). Soybean is broad-leaved. Herbicides that are safe for corn may not be safe for soybeans and vice versa. Herbicides that can be used in both types of crops have real advantage in creating flexibility for the farmer.

Further segmentation is by climate, soil type, and application. Herbicides are more or less effective under different climatic and weather conditions. First is the "macroclimate": Is the weather generally cold or hot, dry or humid? Second is the "microclimate": Was the weather *that year* usually hot or cold, dry or wet, for that particular region? Finally, the method of application is important: liquid spray or dry granular? Farmers with a big investment in equipment for dry application do not switch easily to herbicides that require spray application.

Plummer's test results showed that his new herbicide unequivo-cally outperformed all the competitors' products for corn *and* soy-bean crops in a wide range of soil and weather conditions and spray applications.

Call it serendipity or a form of divine intervention, but Plummer also had another piece of unexpected information. While going through the test fields, where different sections of the field had been sprayed with different companies' herbicide products, he had not-iced that the weeds seemed to fare worst on the boundaries *between* tne sections where his product had been applied and the sections where his competitors' had been applied. Out of curiosity, he had asked for a 50:50 mix of his product and that of his strongest com-petitor to be applied to a test site. When the results came back, they indicated that for most conditions, the combined herbicides outper-formed either individual product. It was this information that was to lead him close to dismissal by Mid-West Chemical, but also to the strategy that would secure him credibility and later spectacular suc-cess in the market.

THE STRATEGY

Intuitively, Plummer knew that he was faced with a situation in which he had neither power nor influence, and his only hope was to find an ally who did. In his analysis of the total situation, he identi-fied a particularly important source of influence: the agricultural colleges. These institutions had significant credibility with his end users, the farmers. They had in place the necessary communication system, the audience needed—all the strategic influence resources he needed to convince the farmers to support his product. Therefore, they could make excellent allies. If he could get them to support his product, and have farmers try the product just once, Rodeo would prove itself in a short time.

The problem was how to package a message that would con-vince a justifiably skeptical audience in the agricultural colleges. It was the solution to this problem that almost got Plummer fired. He asked his research department to conduct numerous ex-periments, with many different combinations of his and the com-petitors' products, to develop a set of optimum *mixes of products* that would do the best job of killing weeds for each major combi-nation of crop, climate, soil, and application condition. Armed with this data, he went to the most influential of the agricultural colleges, arguing that while he admittedly had an interest in sel-ling his product, what he was offering was the combination of his and the competitors' products that was the *best solution to the individual farmer's problem.*

Mid-West Chemical was not amused, initially at least. They pointed out that Plummer's assignment was to sell Rodeo, *not* the competitor's product. Plummer was able to convince them only by arguing that 15 percent of some sales is better than 100 percent of none at all.

To the agricultural colleges, the logic of this argument and the credibility Plummer gained by making the farmers' weed problem the primary focus rather than the sale of Rodeo, were sufficient to convince them to do their *own* testing program. In no time, they were encouraging their audience of farmers to adopt the product mixture approach. In some areas, Plummer's percentage of the recommended mix *was* only 30 percent of the mix, but in many others the mix recommended was 85 percent and even 100 percent Rodeo. In addition, as Plummer had argued to his bosses, the cases where his product was recommended at 30 percent of the mix were cases where before he would not have sold any at all, since a competitor had a better stand-alone product.

Plummer's strategy was not complete without securing the support of another set of stakeholders, the distributors. This group was justifiably disillusioned with the past practice of Mid-West Chemical, which had foisted large inventories of skin irritant on them (in the form of Deadem). Plummer knew that if he could not convince these key players to stock his product, any impact he had on the farmers would be destroyed by distributor hostility. With them he used a double-edged attack. First, he used the same argument he had used with the agricultural colleges: that the mix he was proposing was the *best* solution for the distributor's clients, the farmers. Next, he announced that whereas his predecessors had paid Mid-West's sales force commissions based on pounds of product ordered by distributors, he was going to pay them commission based only on the pounds of herbicide *used* by the farmers. He invented the catch phrase "pounds on the ground" to sell the concept. Furthermore, he argued, just as the sales force was being paid only for herbicide bought by the farmers, so would distributors have to pay only for herbicide they sold to the farmers. In effect, he would sell Rodeo to them on consignment, and there would be a credit and rebill at the end of the season for up to 30 percent of the purchase. Once again, he had intuitively pinpointed the fundamental requirements of the influence play: to communicate *credible* and *strategically appropriate* information to the target audience, and persuade them to act in the way that suited him but also in a way that minimized the risk to them. The distributors bought his argument and stocked the Rodeo.

THE RESULTS

Within three years, the herbicide division was delivering 90 percent of the profits of the entire Mid-West Chemical Company and had gained a major share of the herbicide market. It has done so ever since.

While there is no question that the superiority of the product had the major role to play, Plummer's strategic influence plays did much to break the initial deadlock and accelerate the process. In effect, by astute use of influence, he rapidly turned a fiasco into a triumph.

References

Allison, G. T. *Essence of Decision: Explaining the Cuban Missile Crisis*. Boston: Little, Brown, 1971.

Bacharach, S. B., and E. J. Lawler. *Power and Politics in Organizations*. San Francisco: Jossey-Bass, 1980.

Blau, P. "Differentiation of Power." In *Political Power*, edited by R. Bell, D. V. Edwards, and R. H. Wagner. New York: Free Press, 1969.

Bower, J. H. *Managing the Resource Allocation Process*. Cambridge: Harvard University Press, 1970.

Chamberlain, N. W. *A General Theory of Economic Process*. New York: Harper & Brothers, 1955.

Cohen, H. *You Can Negotiate Anything*. New York: Stuart, 1980.

Crozier, M. *The Bureaucratic Phenomenon*. Chicago: Chicago University Press, 1971.

Cyert, R. M., and J. G. March. *A Behavioral Theory of the Firm*. Englewood Cliffs, N.J.: Prentice-Hall, 1963.

Emerson, R. M. "Power-dependence relations." *American Sociological Review* 27 (February 1962).

Fischer, R., and W. Ury. *Getting to Yes: Negotiating Agreement Without Giving In*. New York: Penguin Books, 1981.

French, J.R.P., Jr., and B. Raven. "The Bases of Social Power." In *Group Dynamics*, 3d ed., edited by D. Cartwright and A. Zander. New York: Harper & Row, 1968.

Guth, W. D., and I. C. MacMillan. "Strategy Implementation Versus Middle Management Self-Interest." Working paper, Center for Entrepreneurial Studies, New York University, 1984.

Hofer, C. W., and D. Schendel. *Strategy Formulation: Analytical Concepts.* St. Paul: West, 1978.

Karass, C. L. *The Negotiating Game.* New York: World Publishing, 1970.

Katz, D., and R. L. Kahn. *The Social Psychology of Organizations.* New York: Wiley, 1966.

Kennedy, J. "Practice and Theory in Negotiations: A Conceptual Model for Negotiations." In *New Directions in Marketing,* edited by R. E. Webster. Proceedings of the 48th National Conference of the American Marketing Association. Chicago: American Marketing Association, 1965.

Lawrence, P., and J. Lorsch. *Organization and Environment.* Boston: Division of Research, Harvard Business School, 1967.

Lederer, W. J., and E. Burdick. *The Ugly American.* New York: Norton, 1958.

MacMillan, I. C. "An Analysis of Certain Power and Influence Relations between the Firm and its Environment." Master's thesis, University of South Africa, 1972.

MacMillan, I. C. "Preemptive Strategies." *Journal of Business Strategy* 4(2) (Fall 1983): 16–26.

MacMillan, I. C., and W. D. Guth. "Strategy Implementation and Middle Management Coalitions." In *Advances in Strategic Management, vol. 3,* edited by R. Labm. Greenwich, Conn.: JAI Press, 1985.

MacMillan, I. C., M. L. McCaffery, and G. L. Van Wijk. "Competitive Responses to Easily Initiated New Products." *Strategic Management Journal* 6(1) (1985): 75–86.

March, J. G., and H. A. Simon. *Organizations.* New York: Wiley, 1957.

Marchal, J. "The Construction of a New Theory of Profit." *American Economic Review* 41, (4) (1951).

Maslow, A. H. *Motivation and Personality.* New York: Harper & Row, 1954.

McGregor, D. *The Human Side of Enterprise.* New York: McGraw-Hill, 1960.

Parsons, T. C. *Politics and Social Structure.* New York: Free Press, 1969.

Pettigrew, A. M. *The Politics of Organizational Decision-Making.* London: Tavistock, 1973.

Pfeffer, J. *Power in Organizations.* Marshfield, Mass.: Pitman, 1981.

Pfeffer, J., and G. R. Salancik. *The External Control of Organization.* New York: Harper & Row, 1978.

Porter, M. E. *Competitive Strategy: Techniques for Analyzing Industries and Competitors.* New York: Free Press, 1980.

Rappaport, A. *Fights, Games, and Debates.* Ann Arbor: University of Michigan Press, 1960.

Riker, W. H. *The Theory of Political Coalitions.* New Haven: Yale University Press, 1962.

Schein, E. H. *Organizational Psychology.* Englewood Cliffs, N.J.: Prentice-Hall, 1963.

Schelling, T. C. *The Strategy of Conflict.* Cambridge: Harvard University Press, 1963.

Schumpeter, J. A. *Capitalism, Socialism and Democracy.* New York: Harper Brothers, 1942.

Thompson, J. D. *Organizations in Action.* New York: McGraw-Hill, 1967.

Tichy, N. M. *Managing Strategic Change.* New York: Wiley, 1983.

Tushman, M. L. "A Political Approach to Organizations: A Review and Rationale." *Academy of Management Review* 2 (1977).

Walton, R. E., and R. B. McKersie. *A Behavioral Theory of Labor Negotiations.* New York: McGraw-Hill, 1969.

Index

0–314–85260–3